AF241142

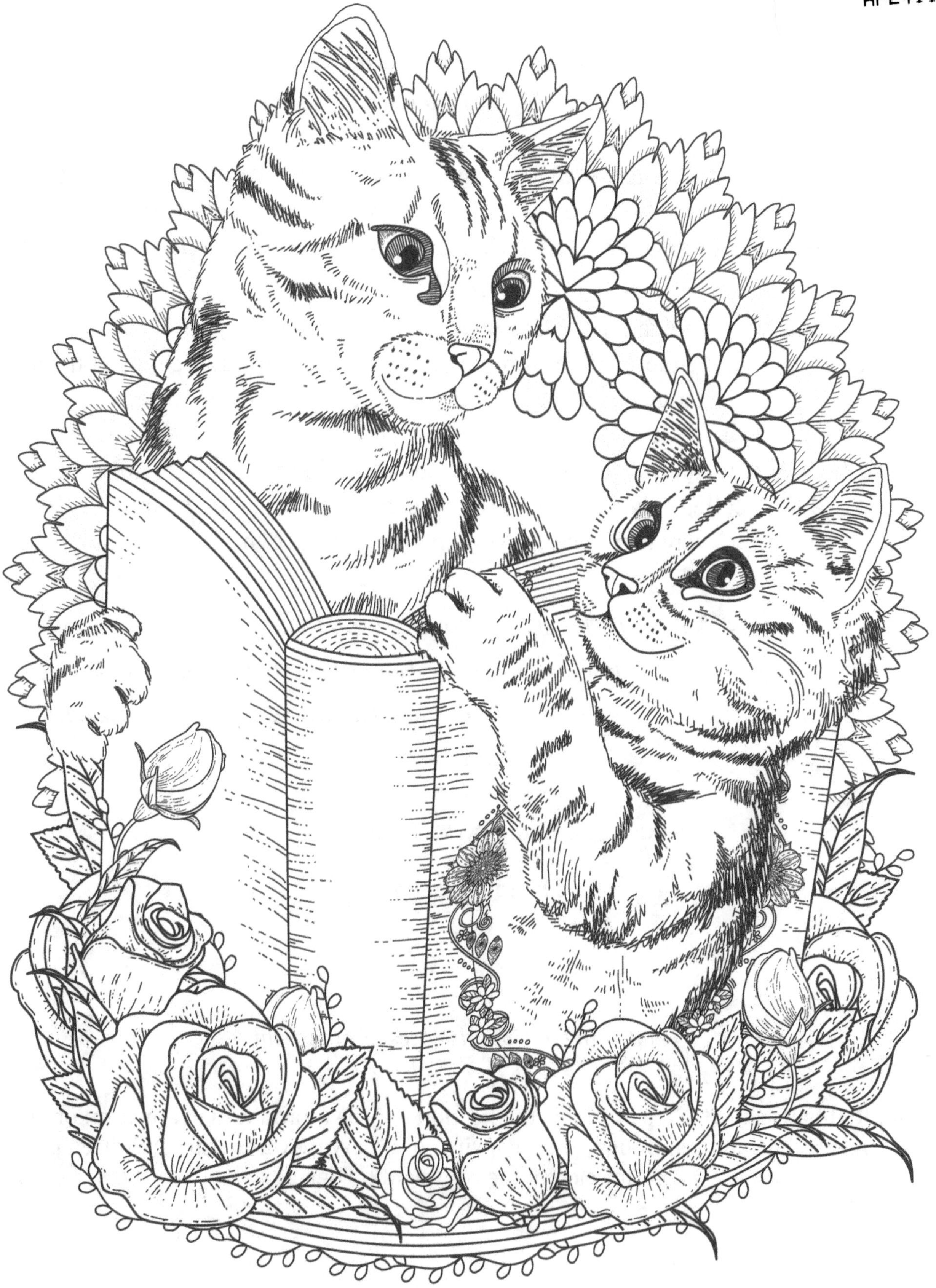

Colorful Cats for Kid
A Stress Relieving Cat Book Design for Kid

It is time you relax and let the creativity flow through you. Step away from everyday life stress by taking Your Coloring to the Next Level - Learn the Art of Coloring and Achieve the Ultimate Bliss!

Bring out your imagination, arouse your senses and creativity, and as you become engaged in the pleasurable, soothing activity of Coloring, it calms you and instantaneously starts reducing your stress level.

This book is a wonderful addition to your coloring library; a perfect gift school aged children, college students, or adults who enjoy coloring, and a much easier way to reduce stress than going to the gym.

THANKS YOU FOR YOUR PATRONAGE

I love hearing your feedback and I read every single review

Please send your comment, ideas, compliments and anything else to me at:

stevojionu@gmail.com

Printed in the United States of American

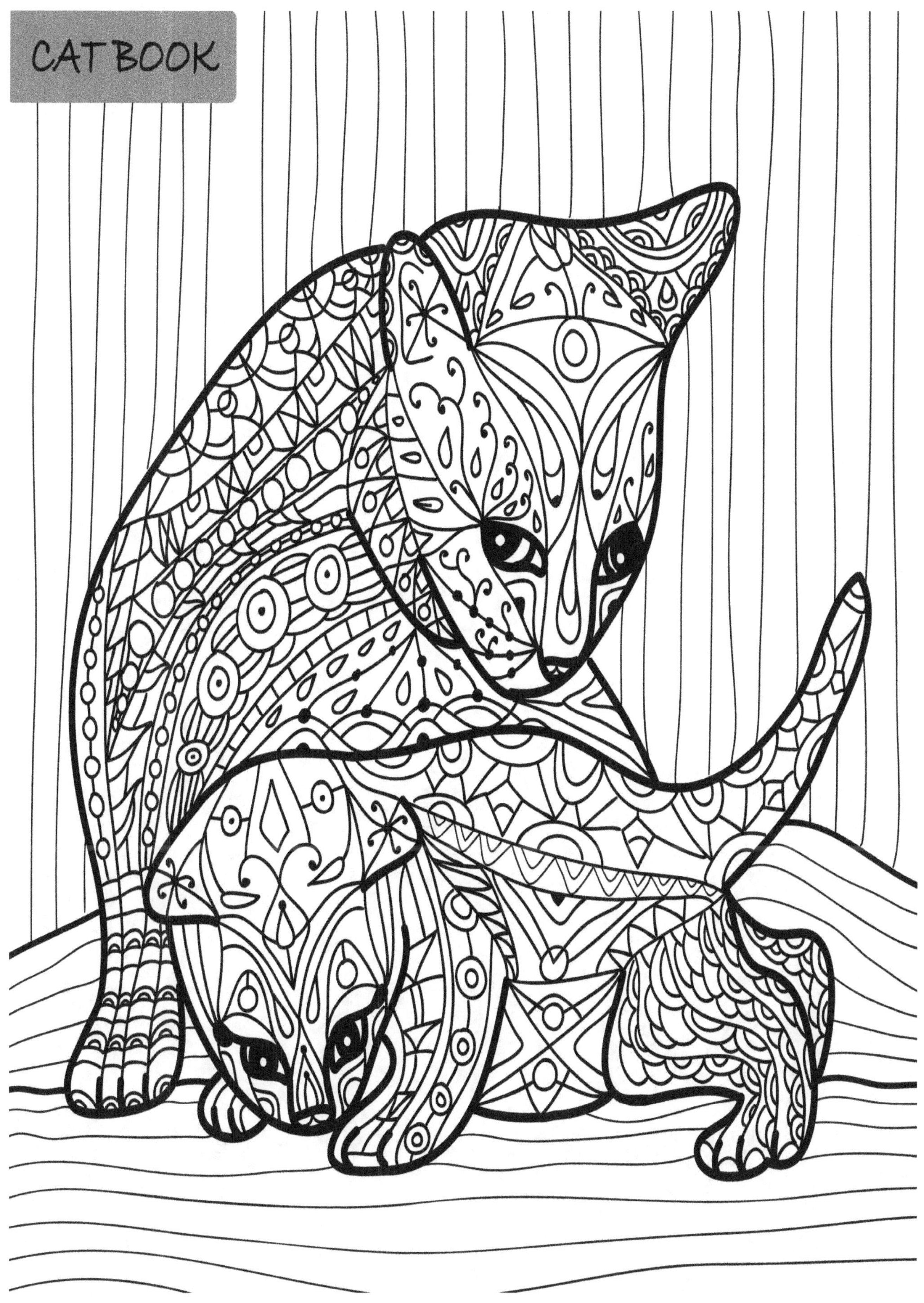
CAT BOOK

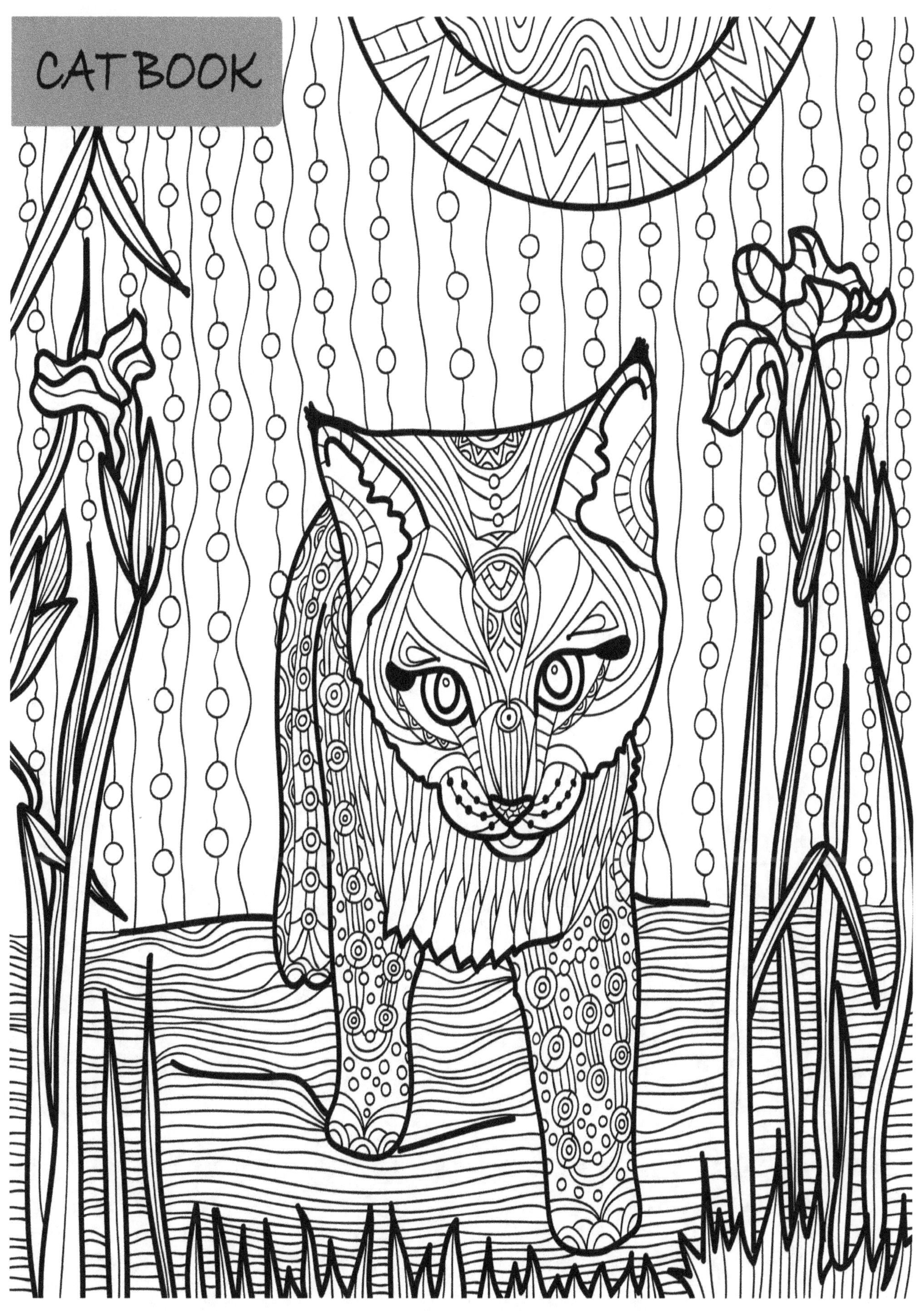
CAT BOOK

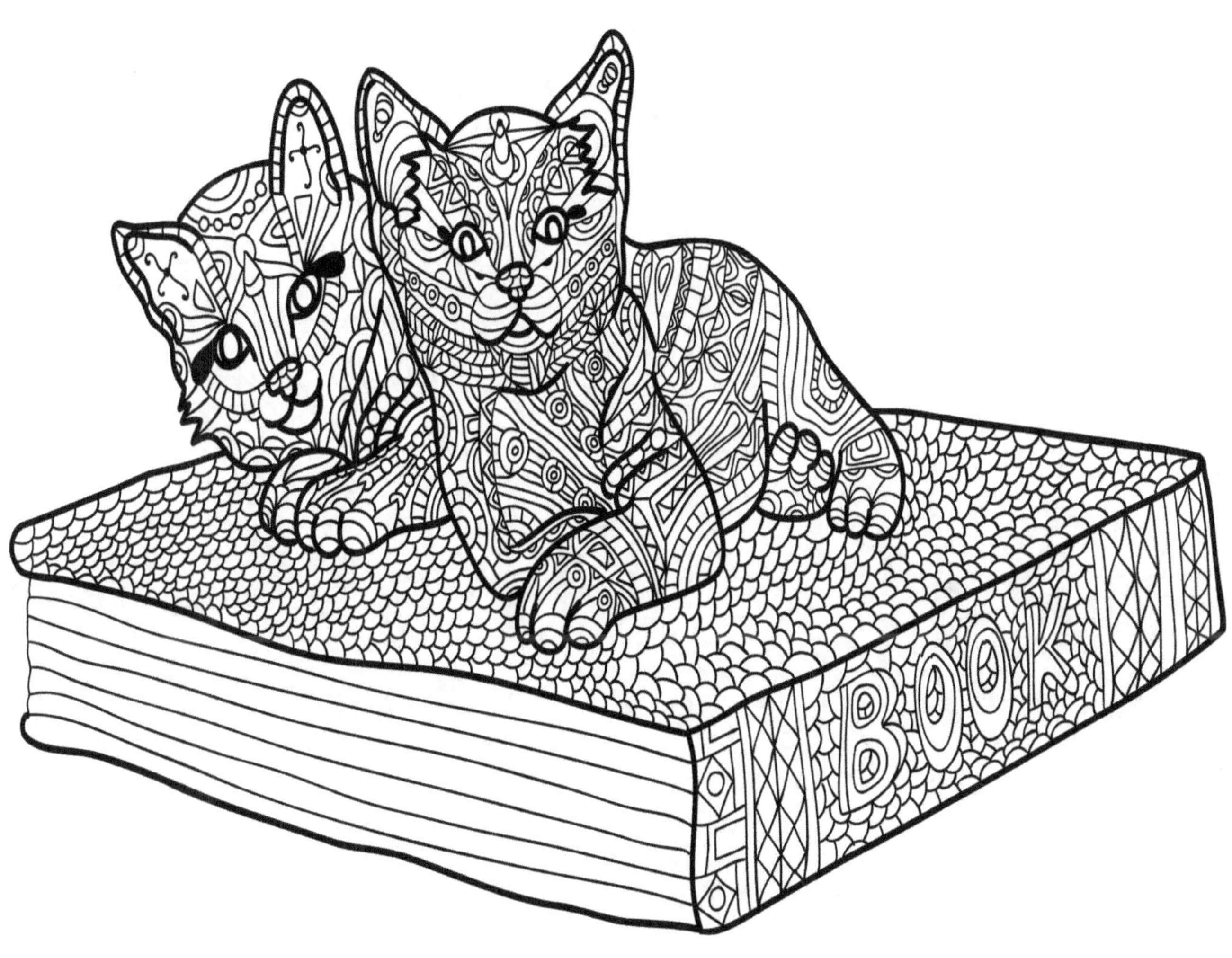

BOOK

CAT BOOK

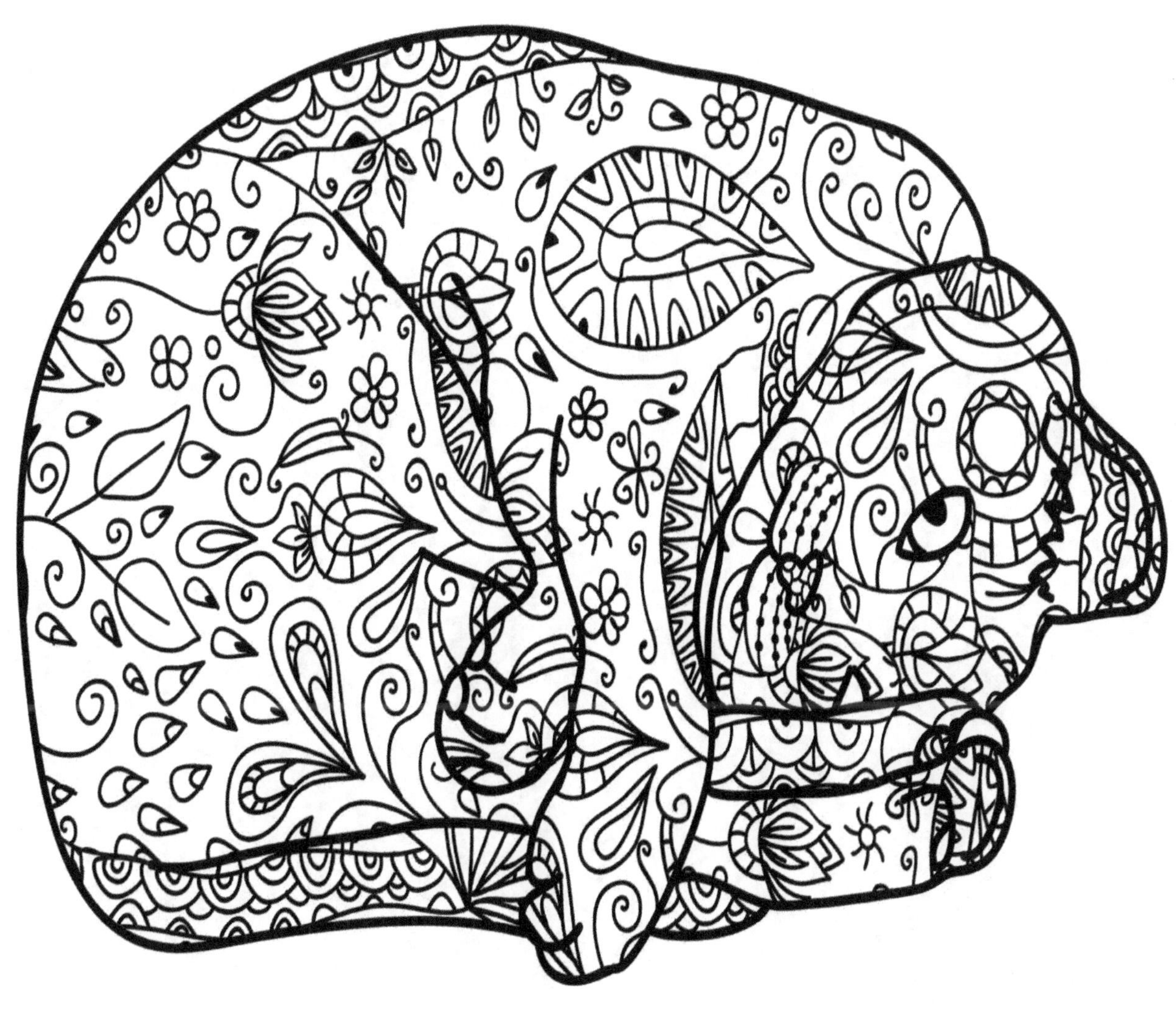

CAT BOOK

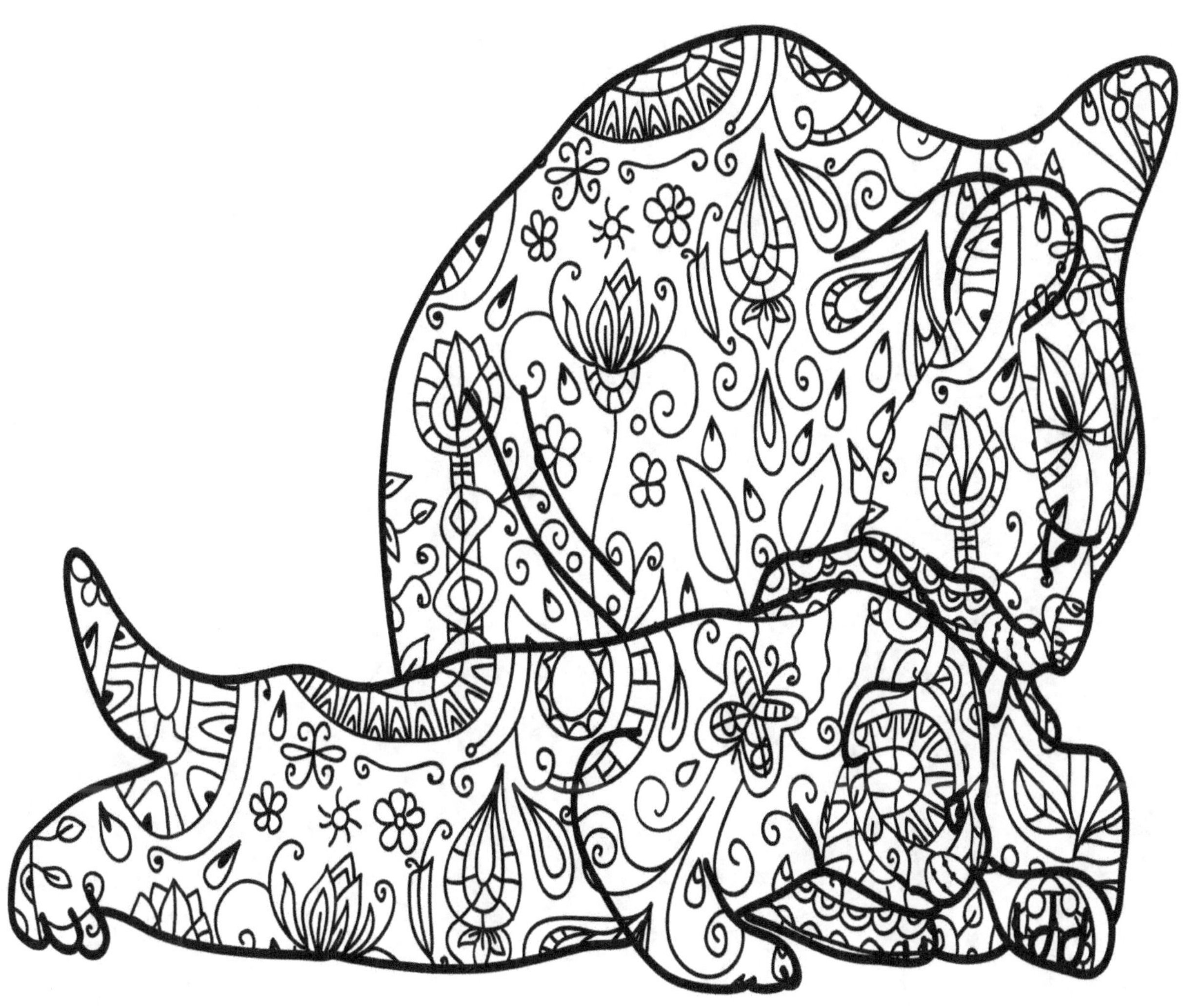

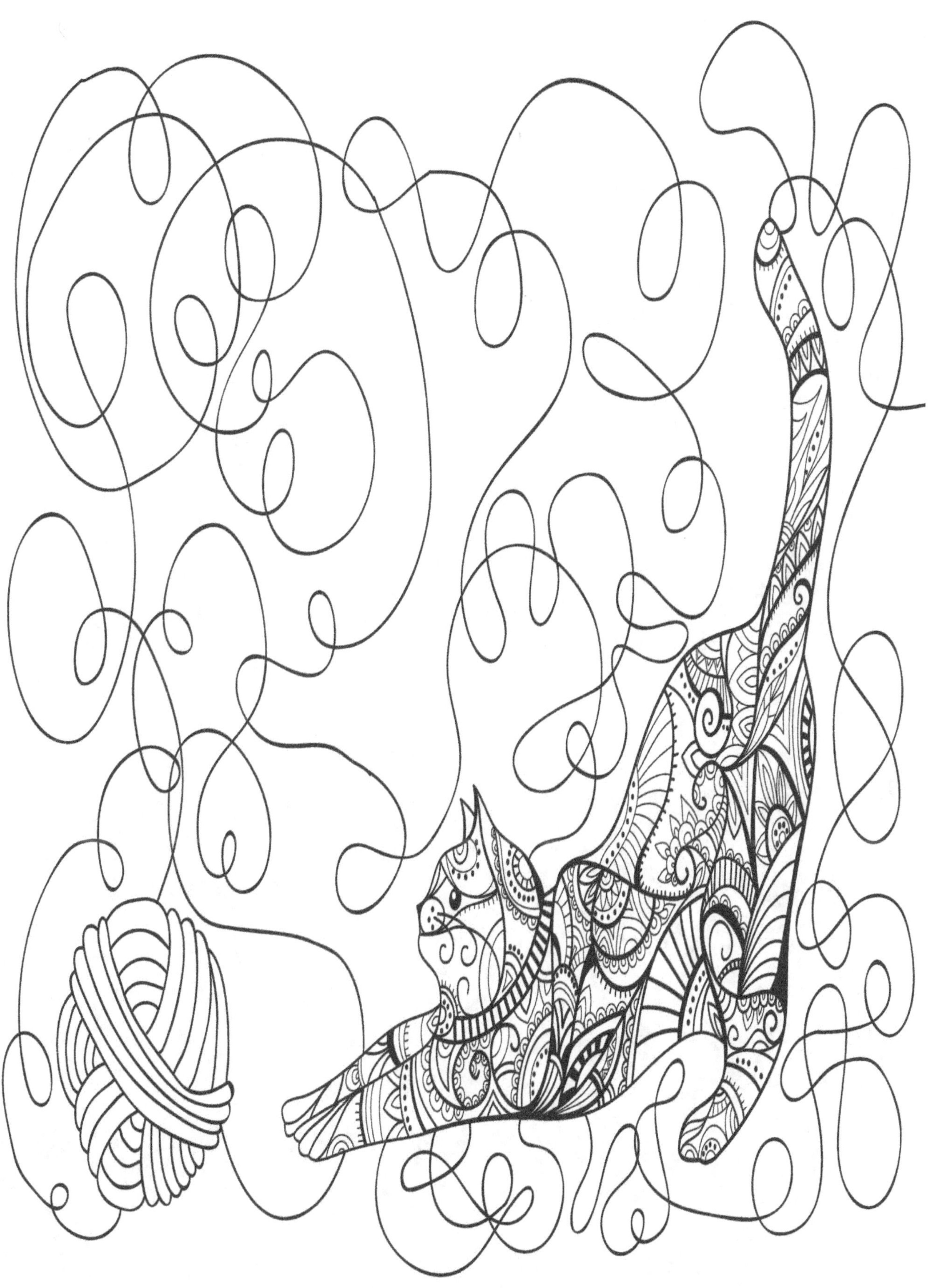

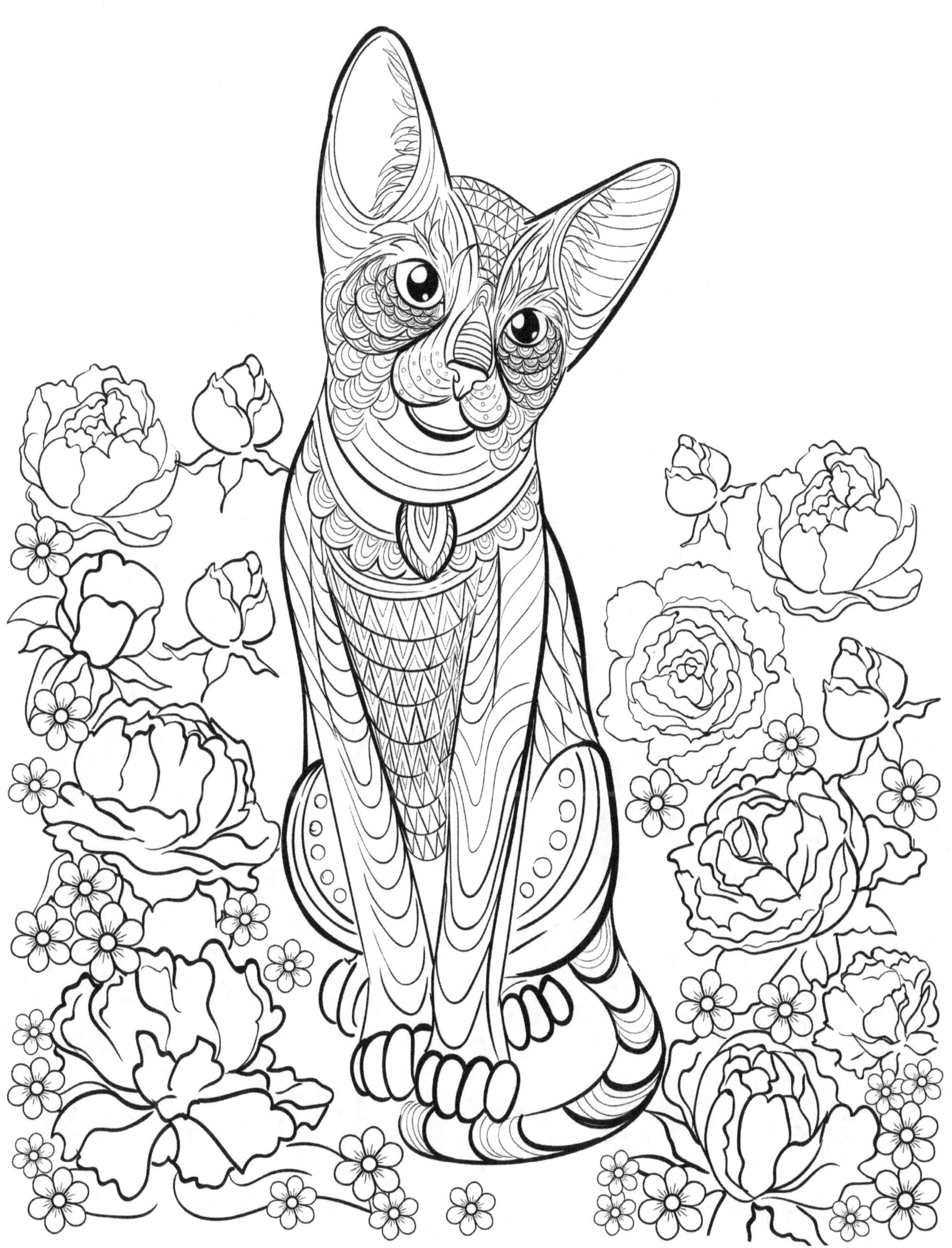

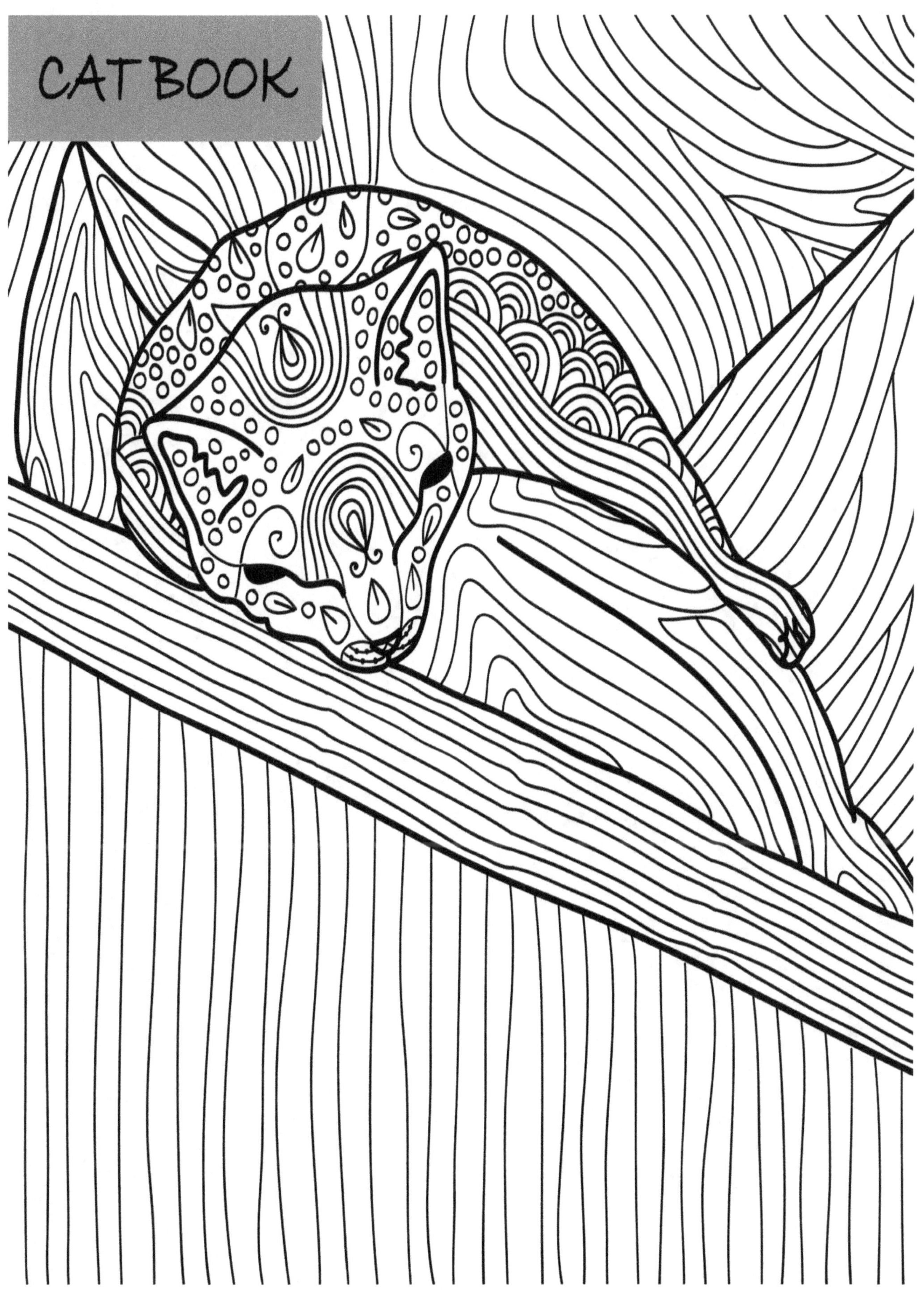

CAT BOOK

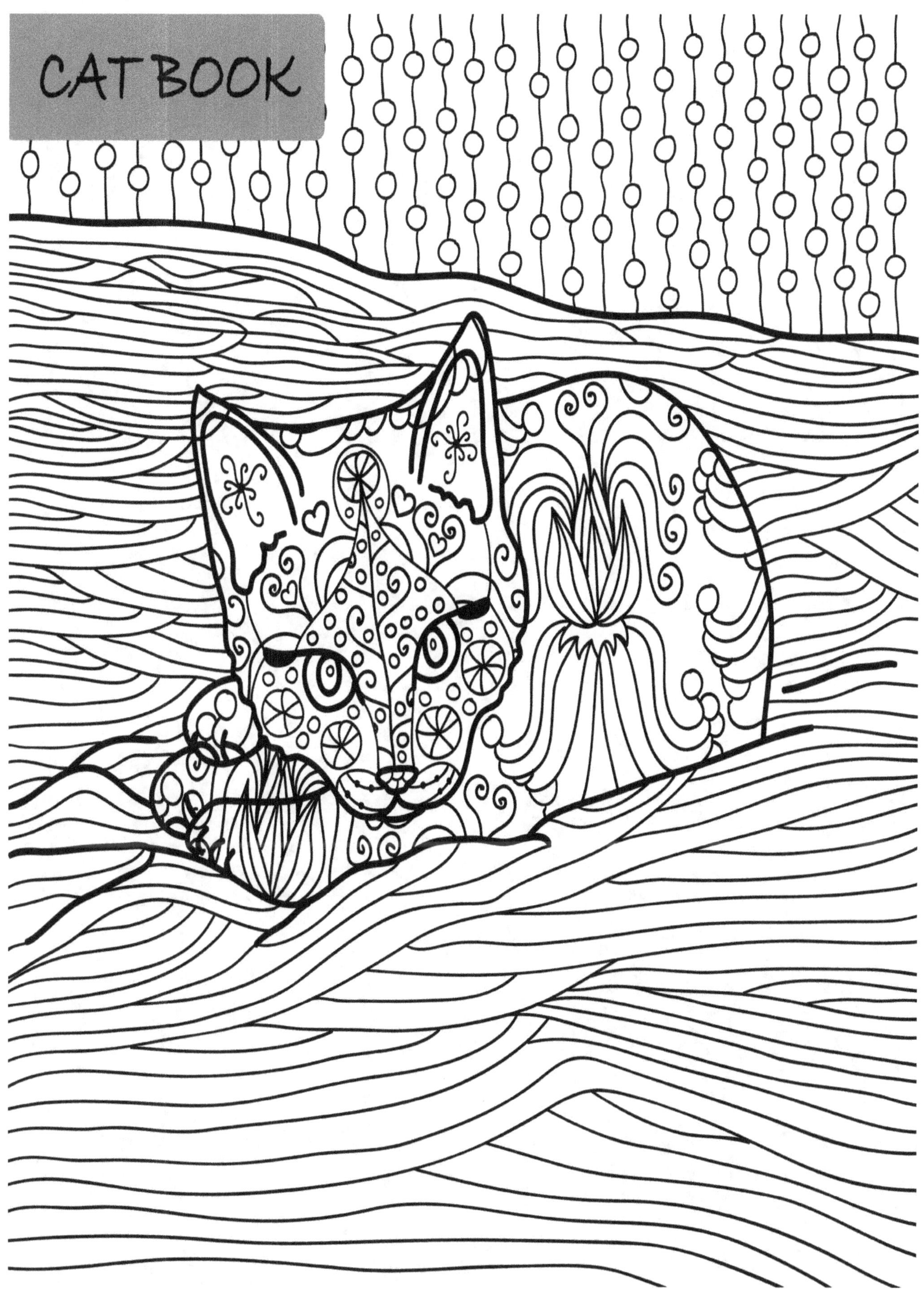
CAT BOOK

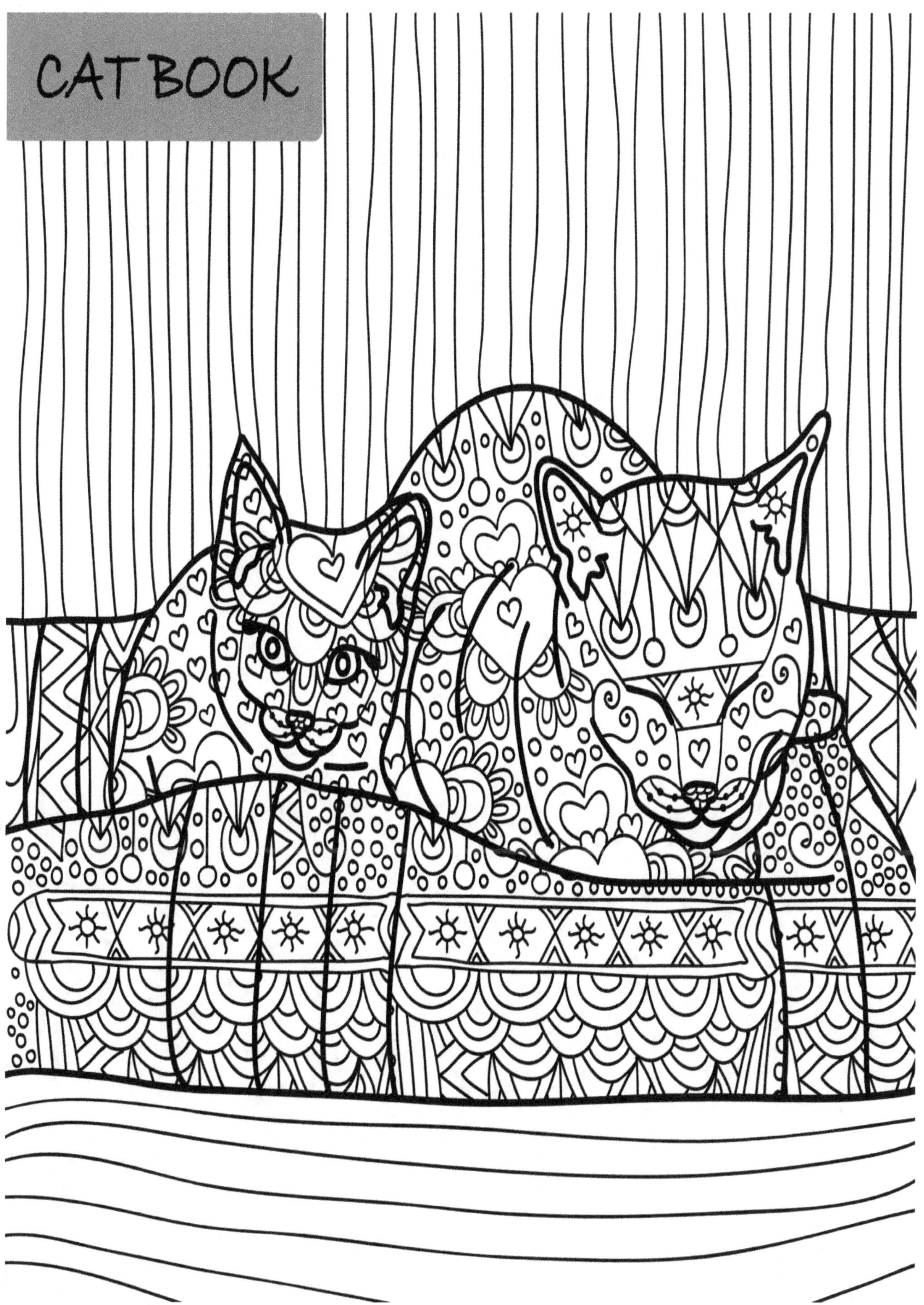
CAT BOOK

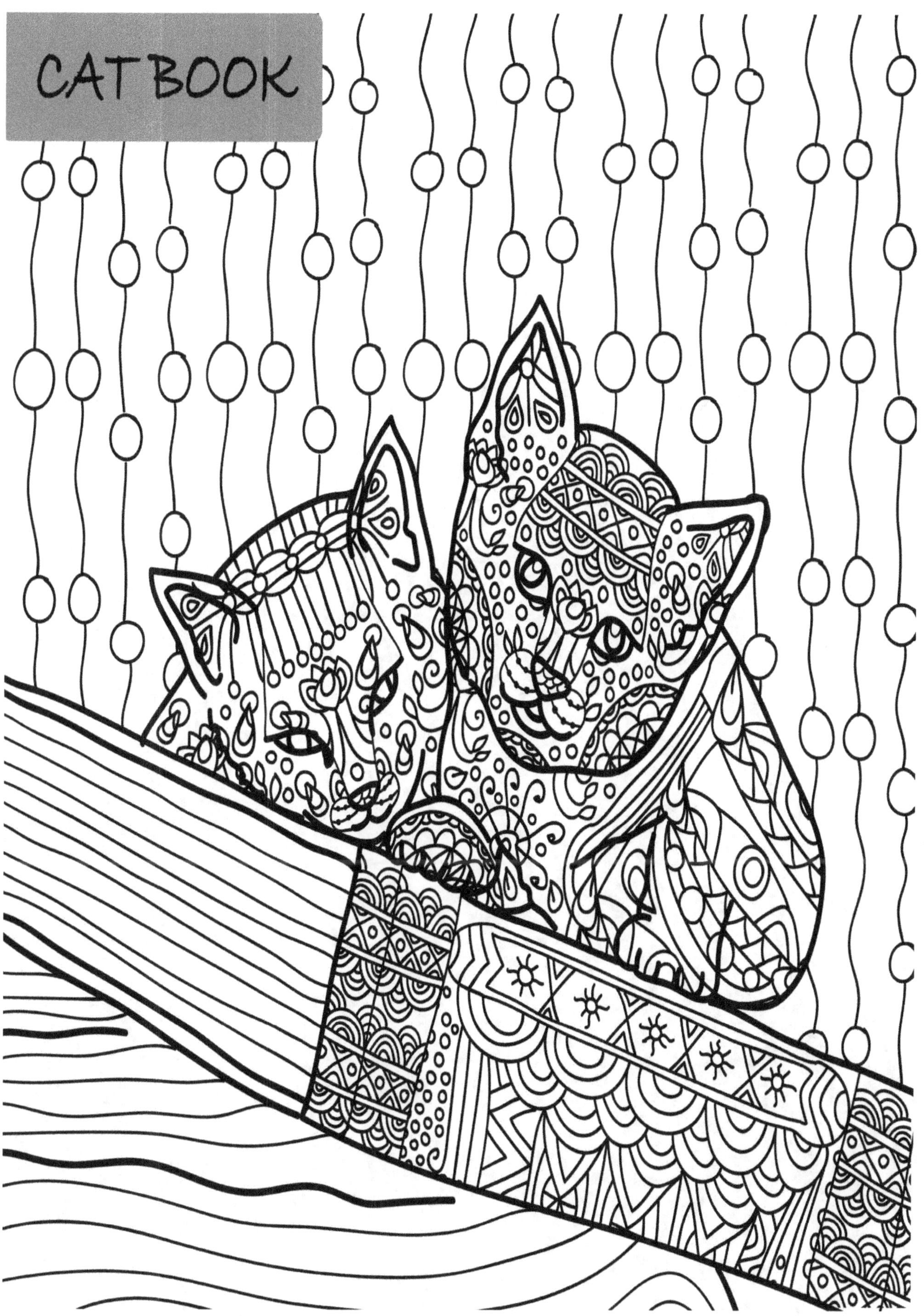
CAT BOOK

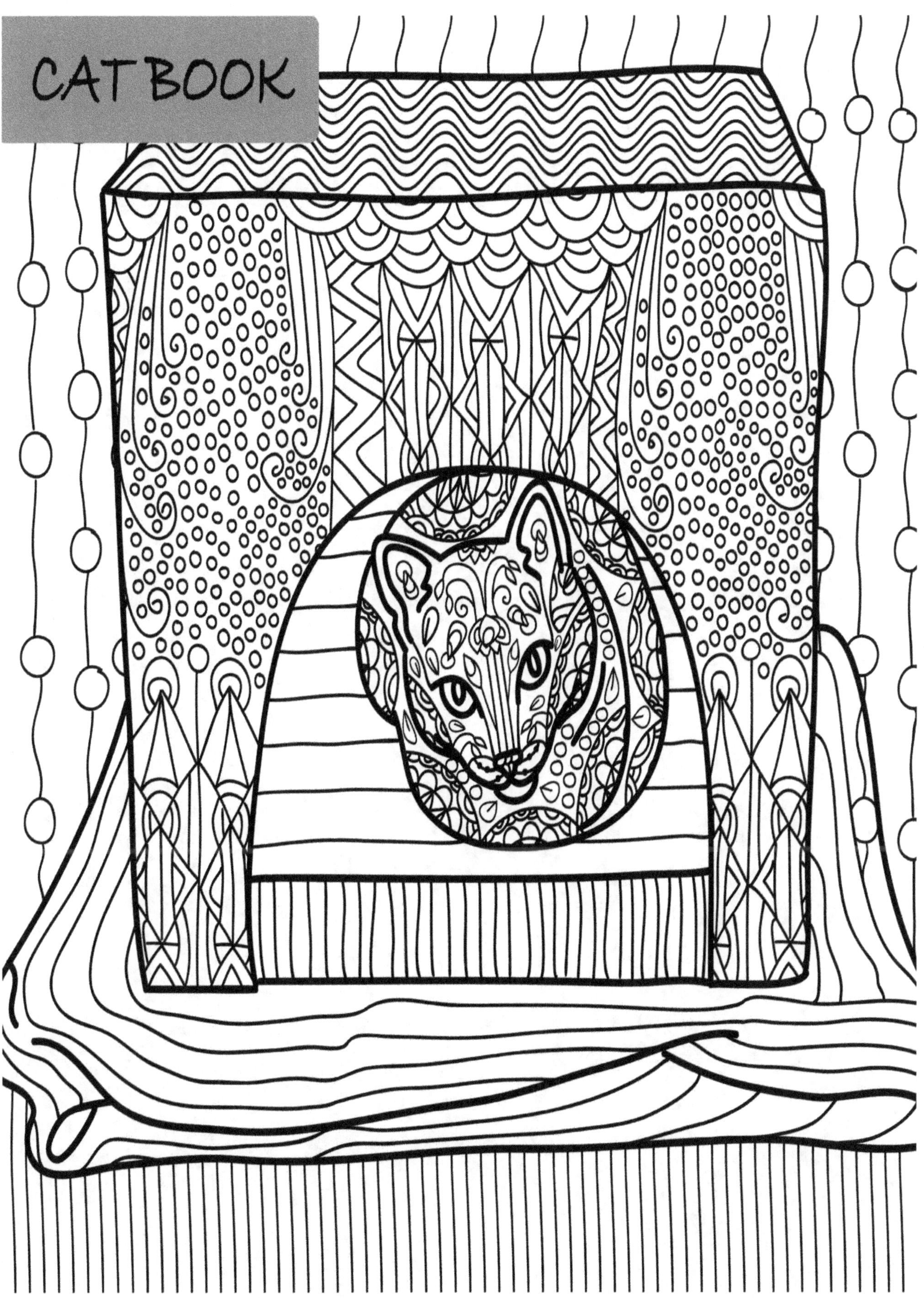
CAT BOOK

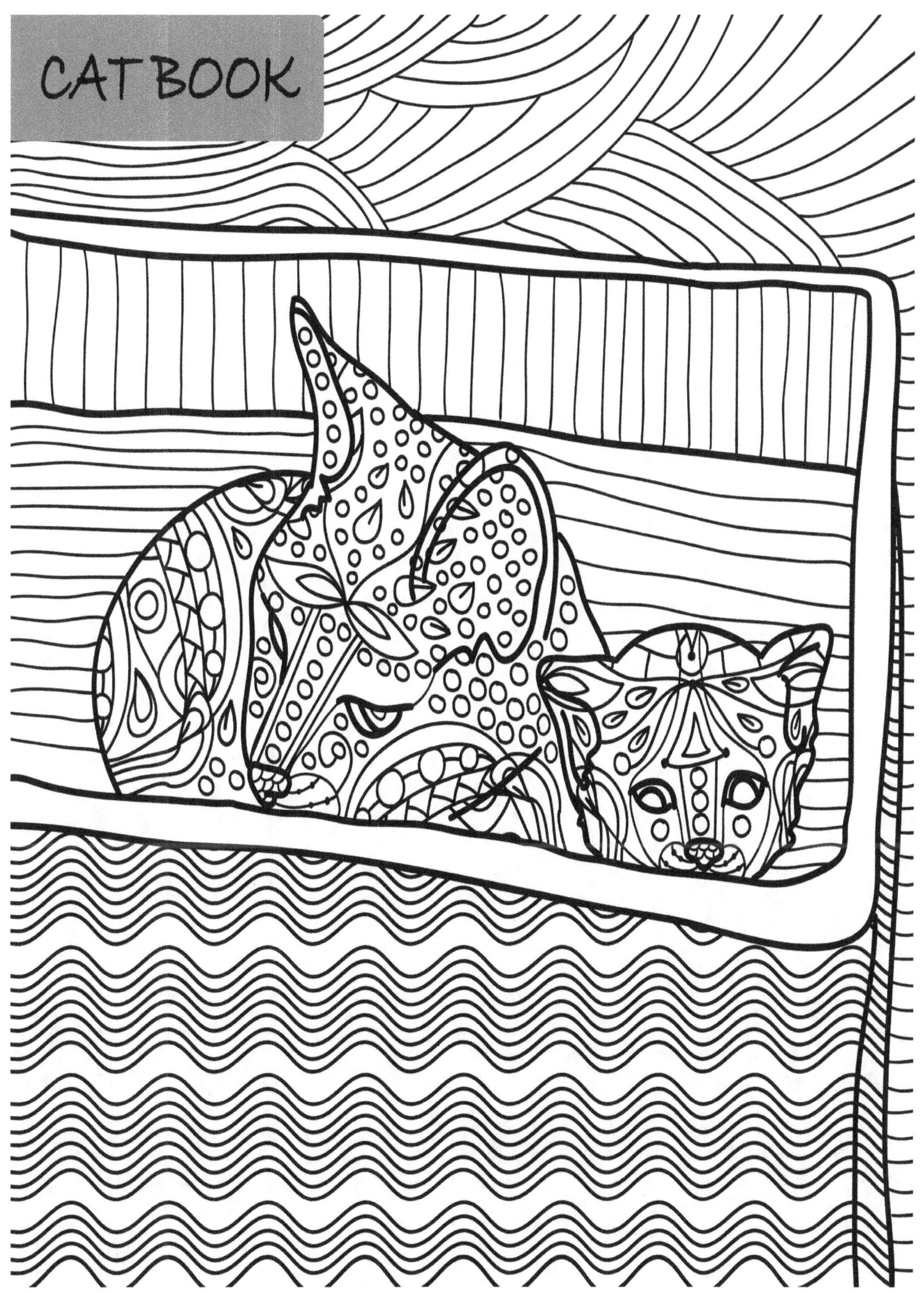CAT BOOK

CAT BOOK

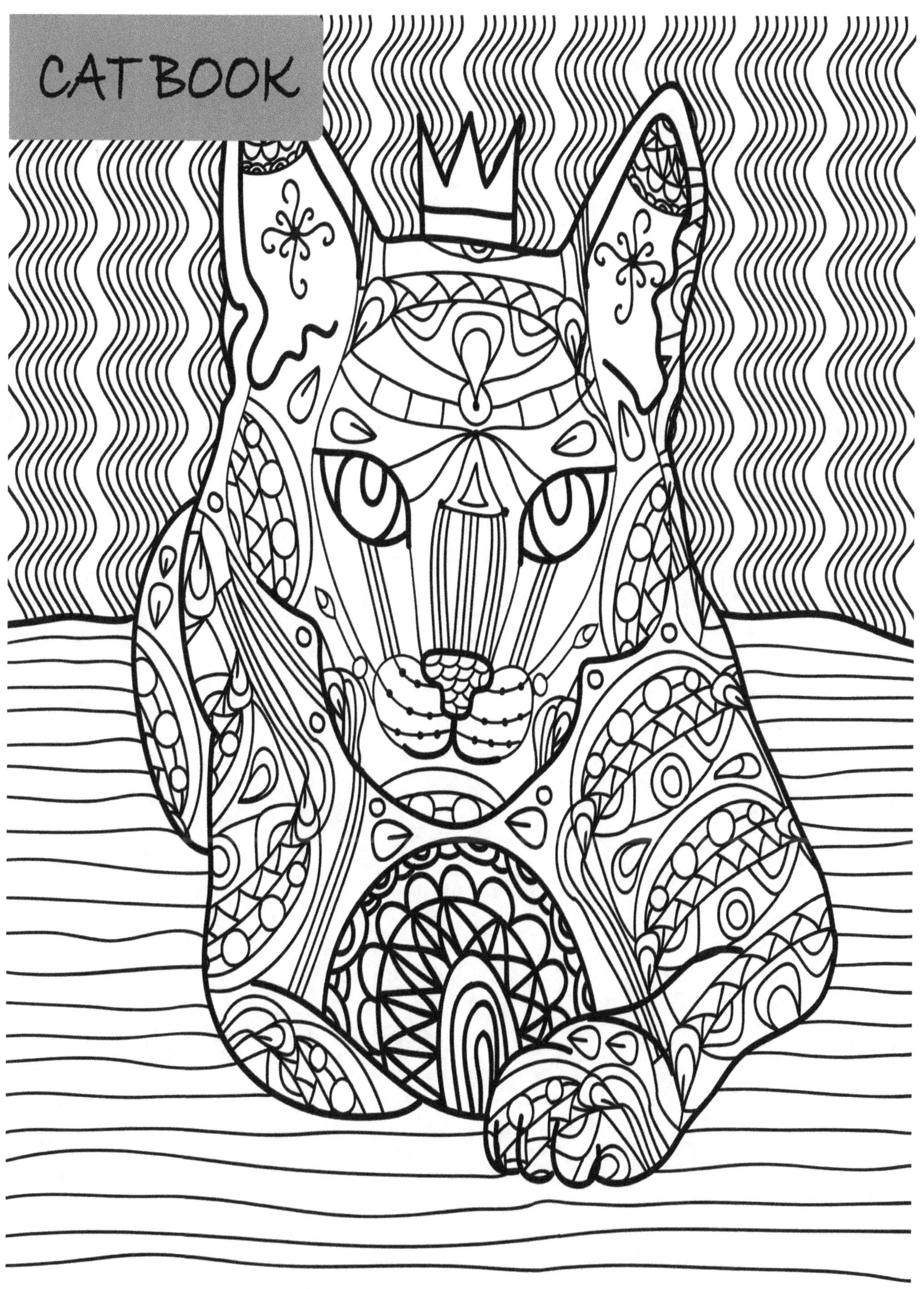

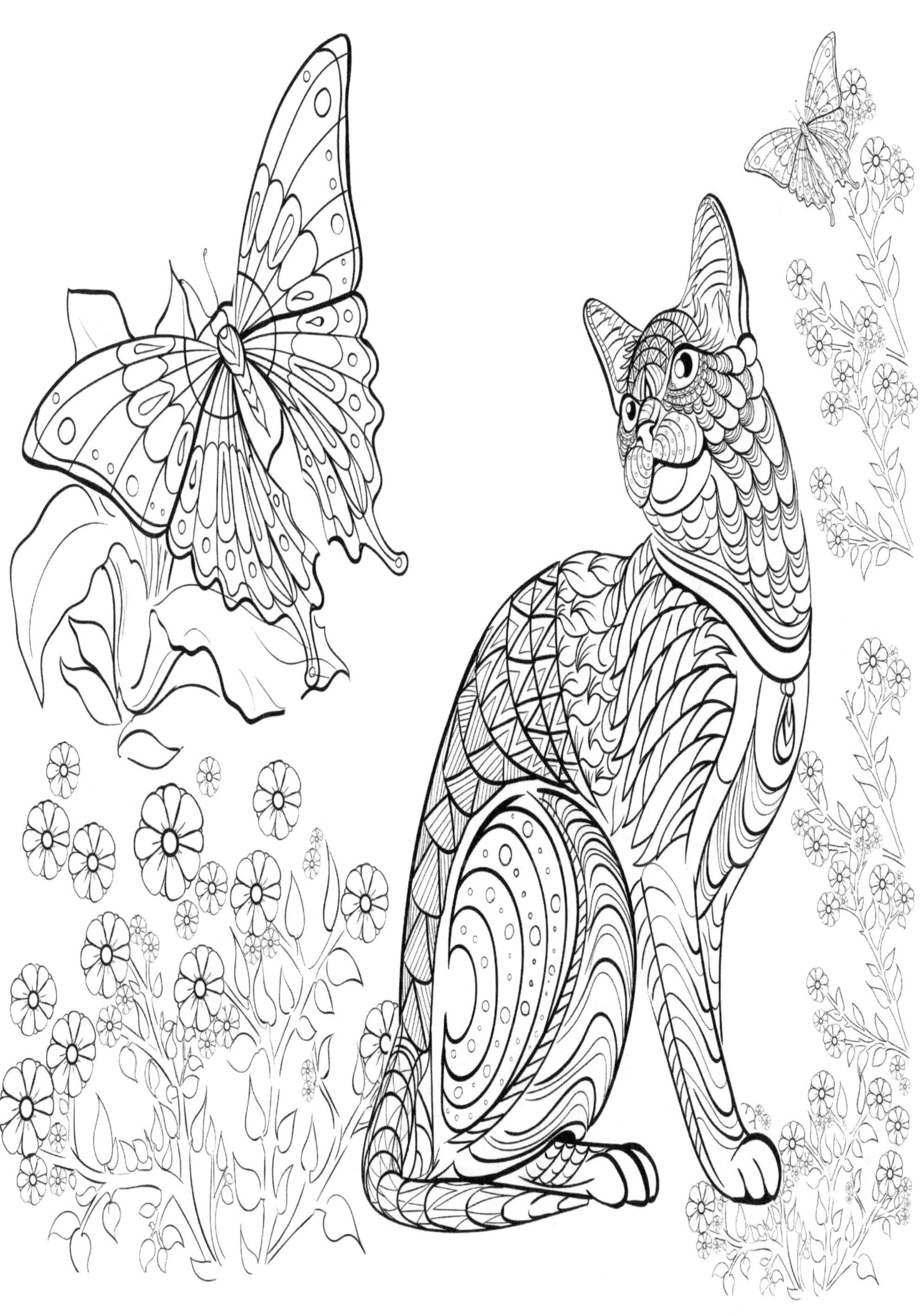

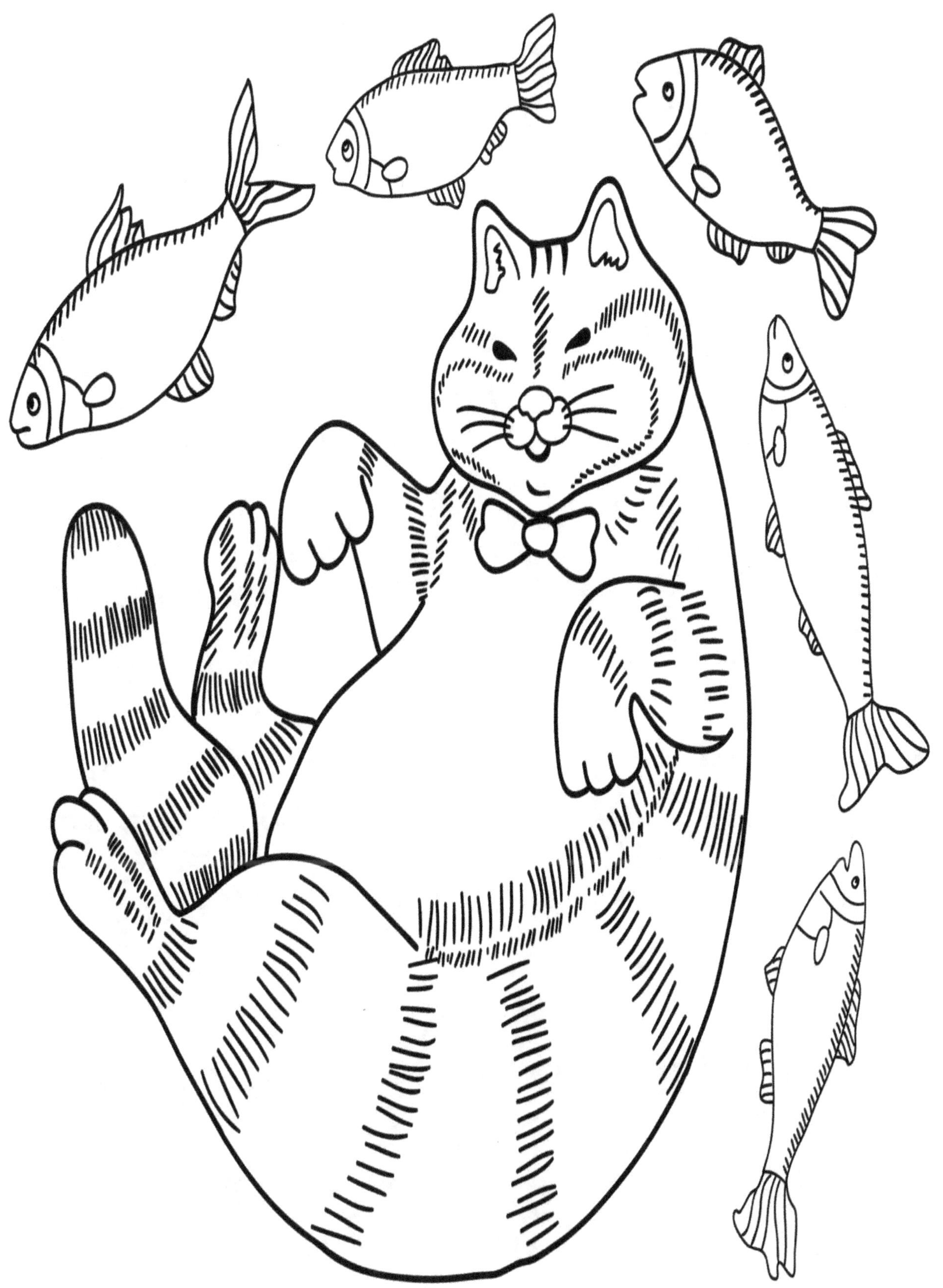

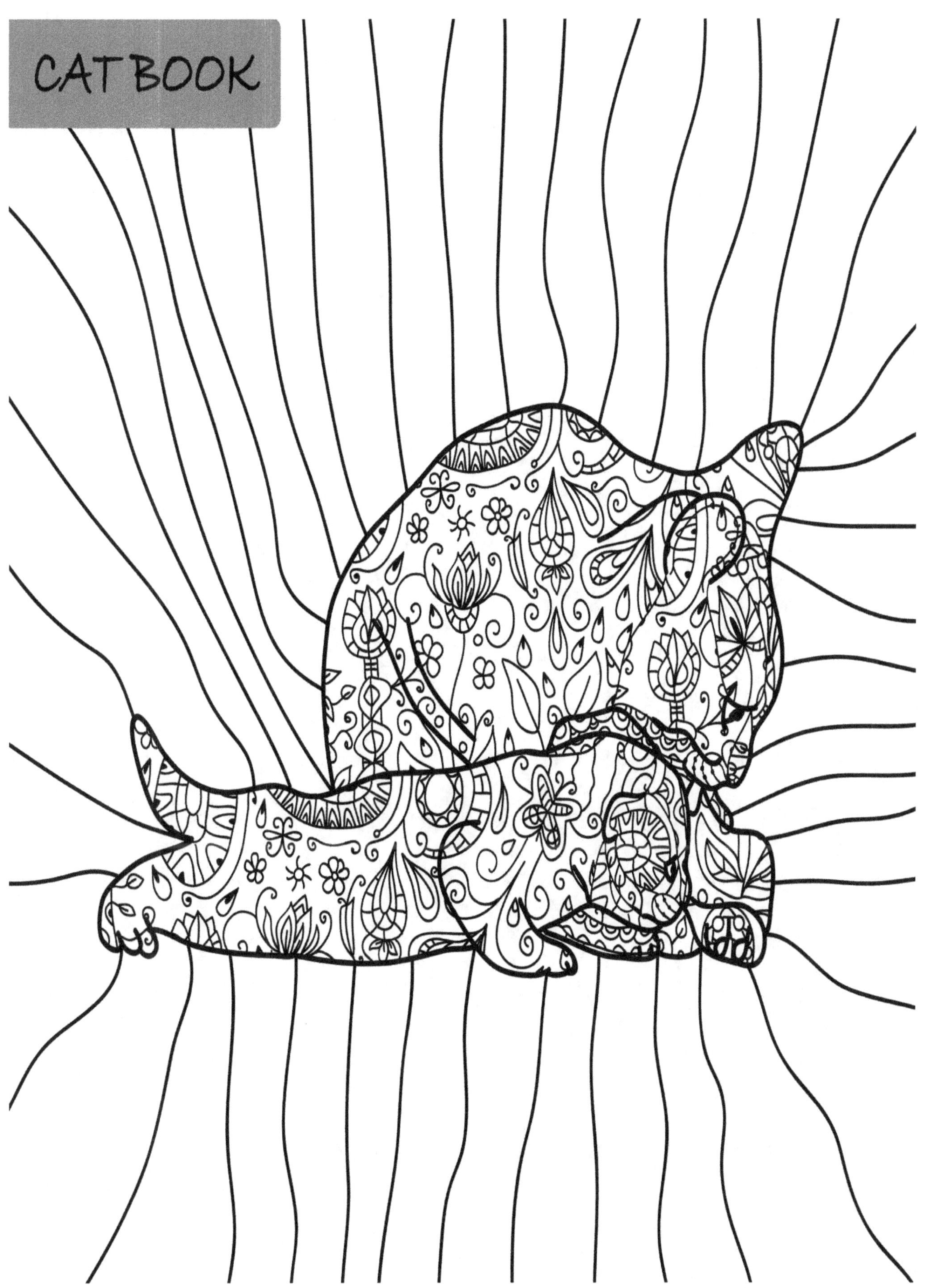
CAT BOOK

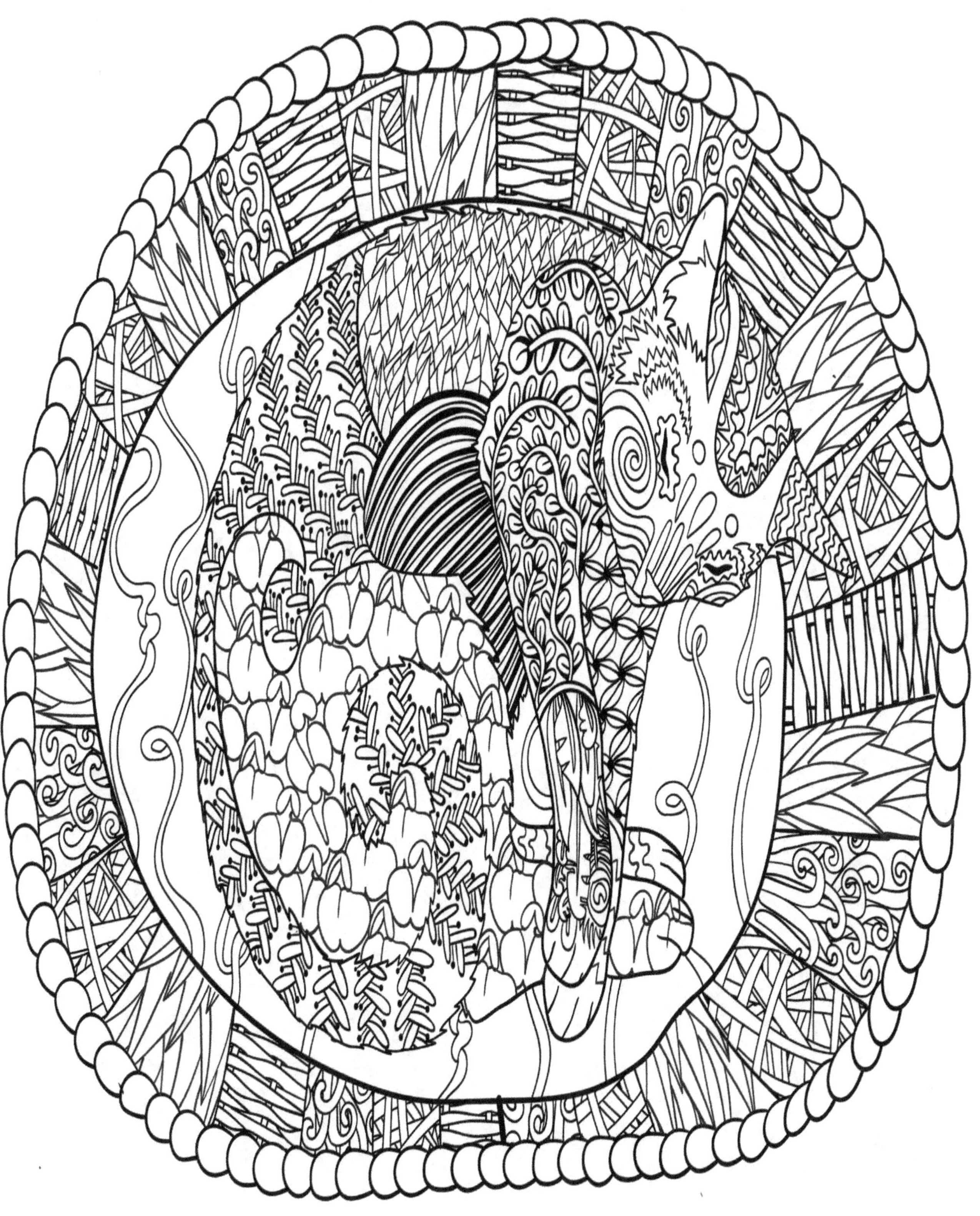

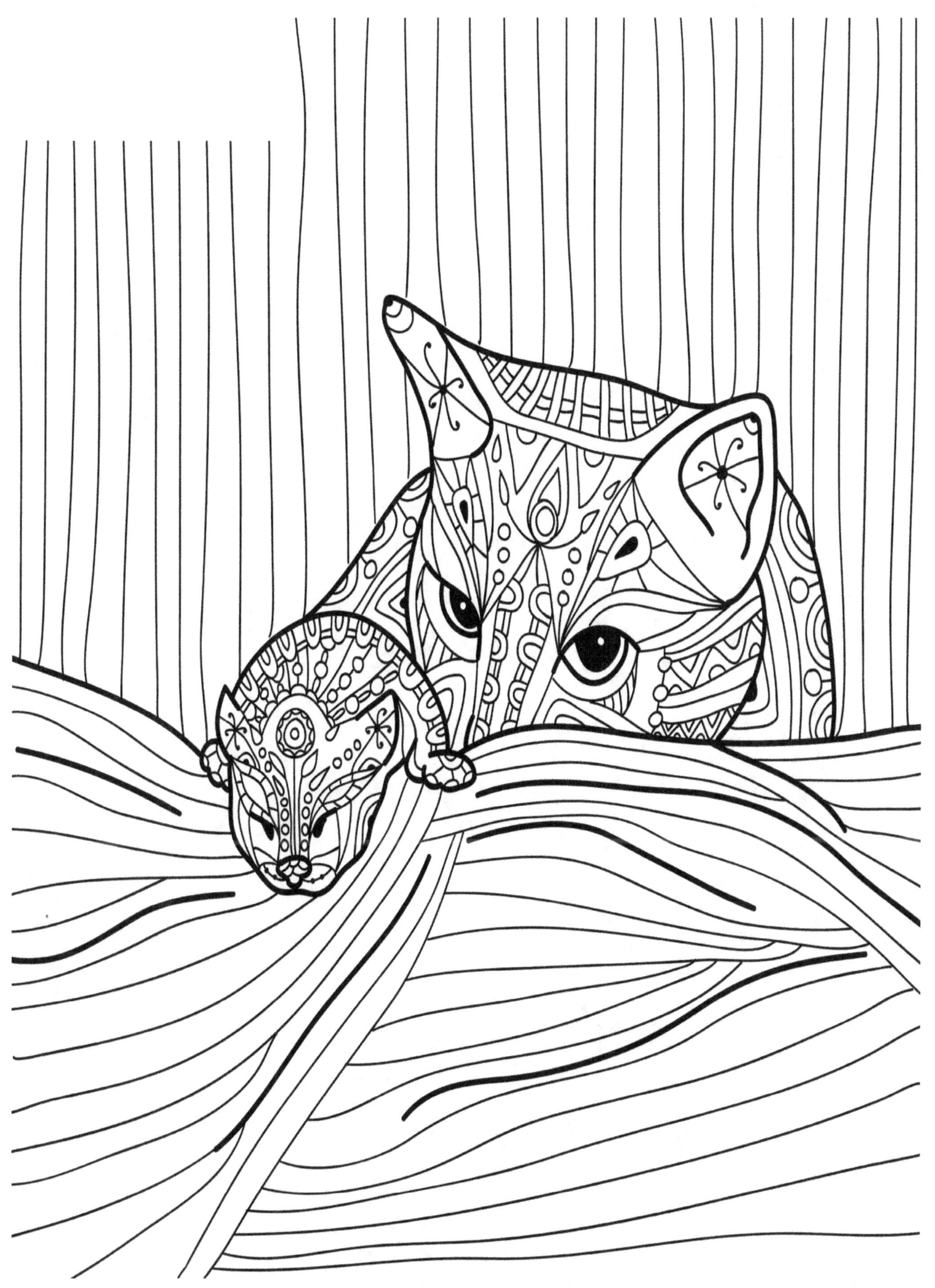

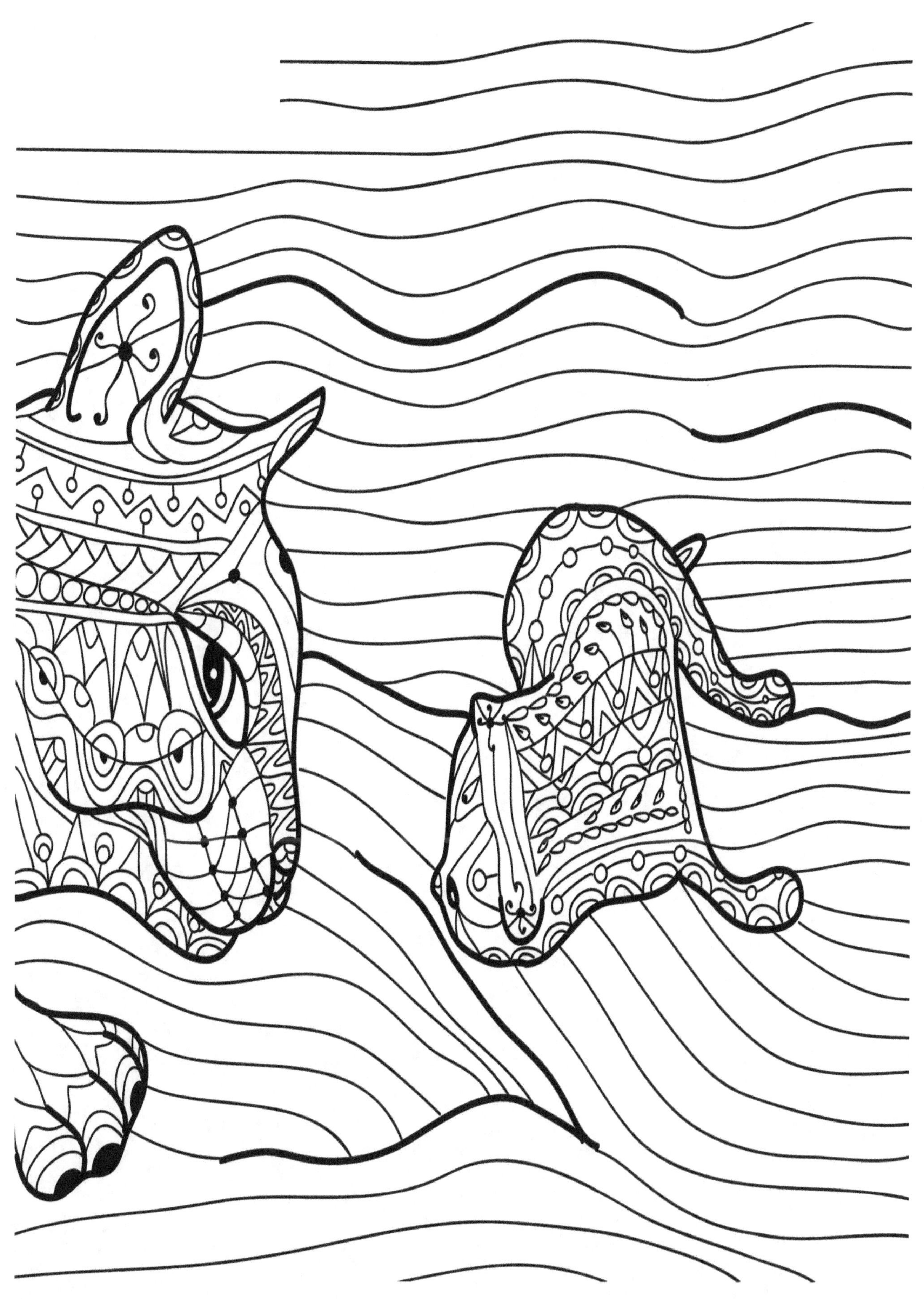

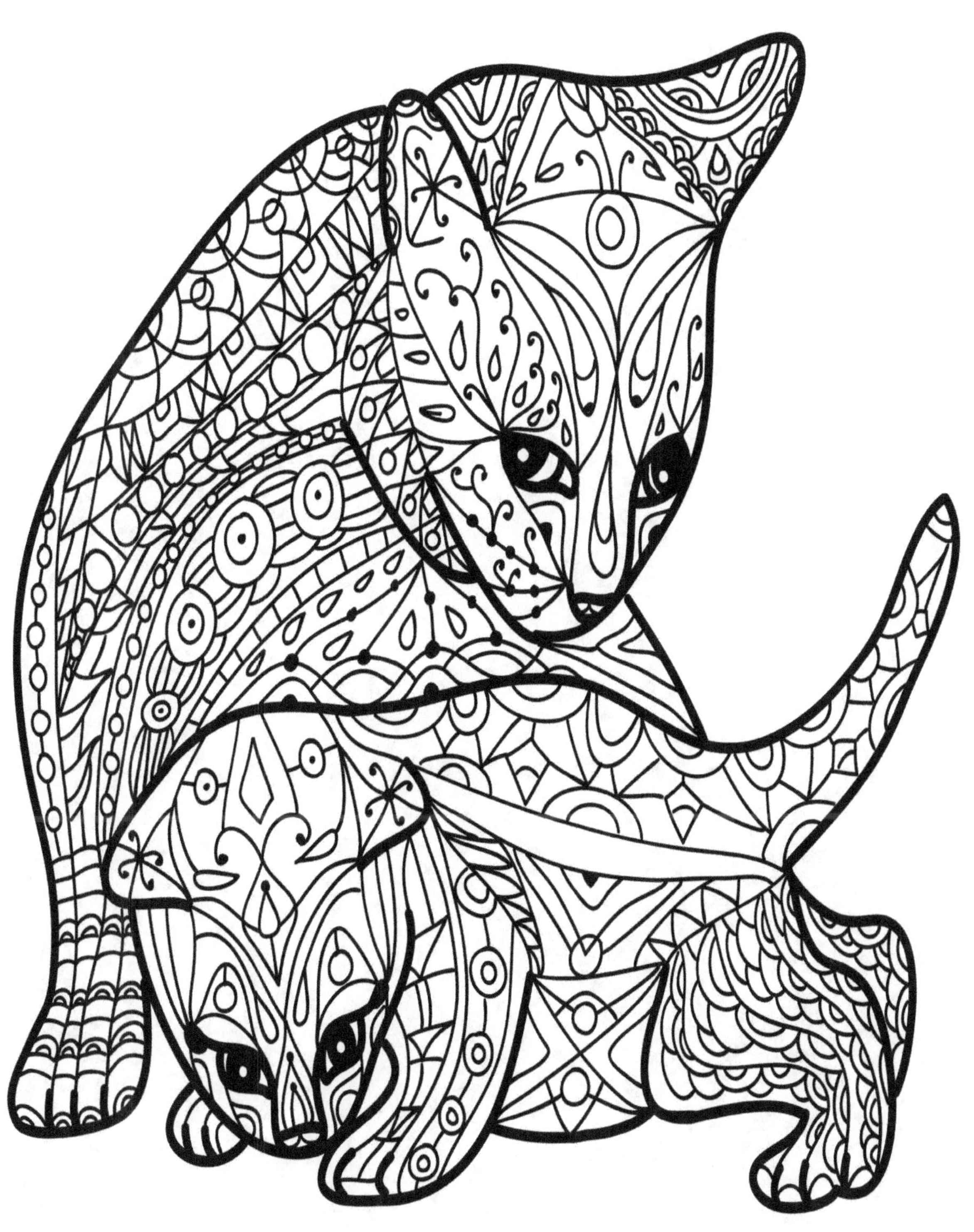

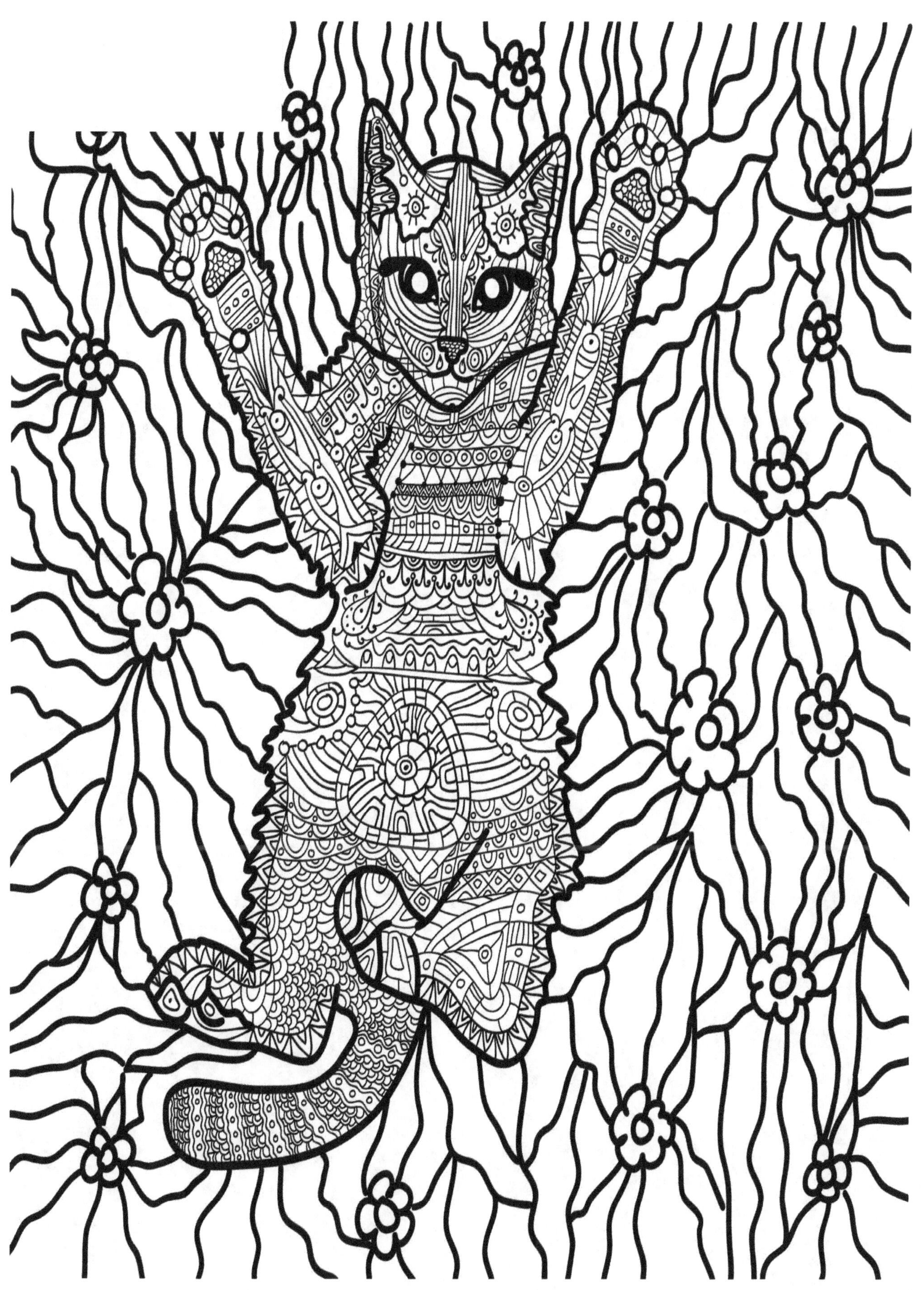

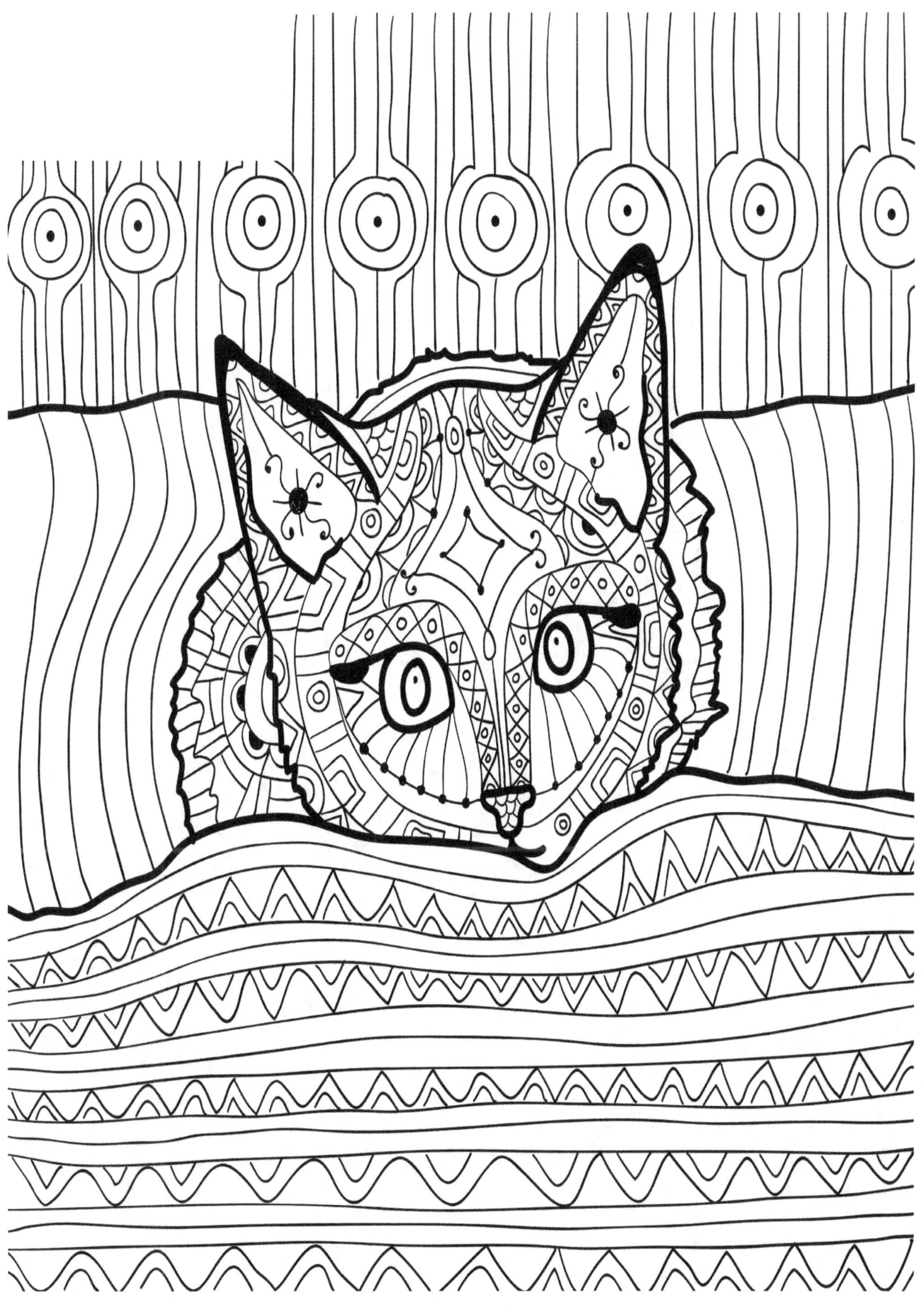

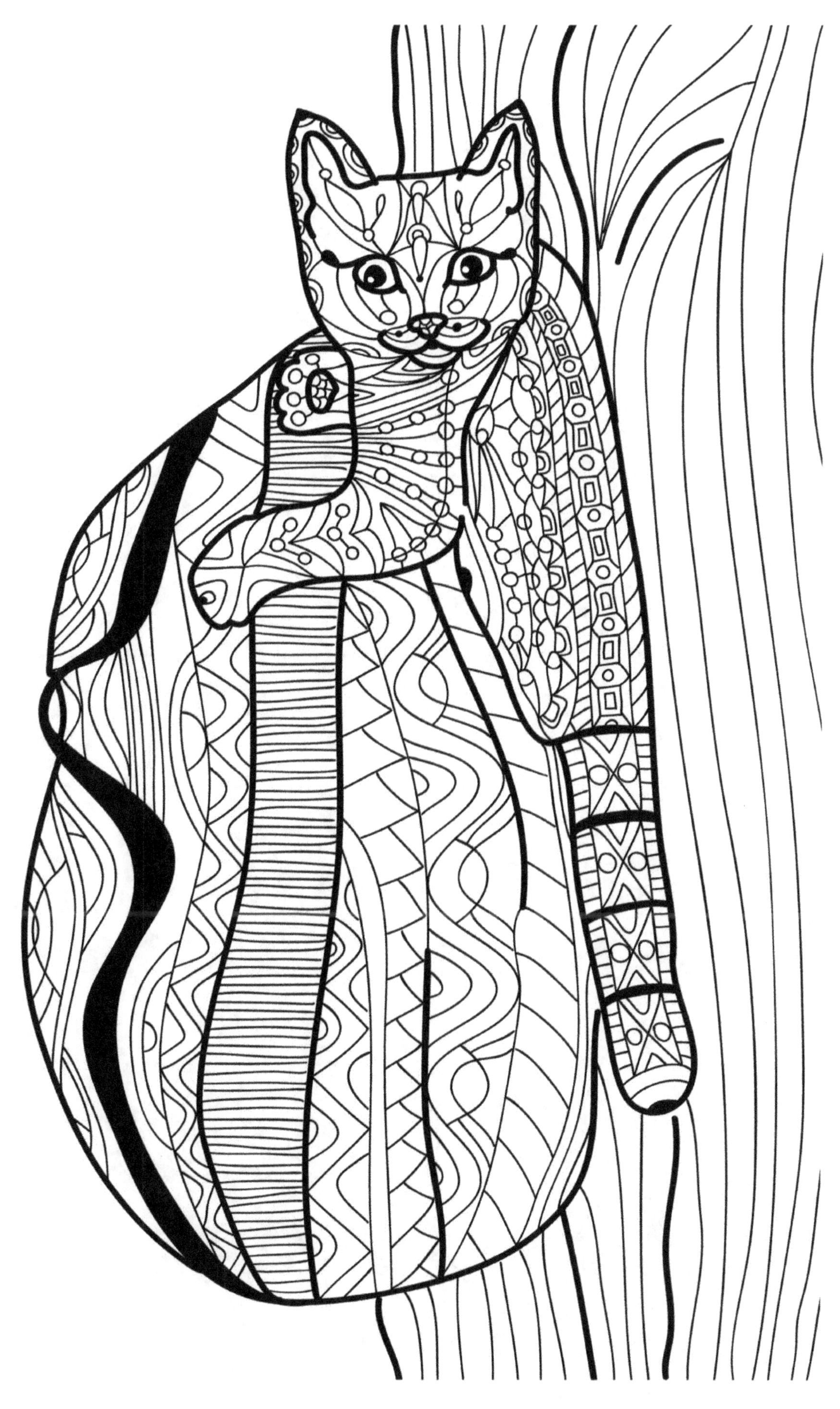

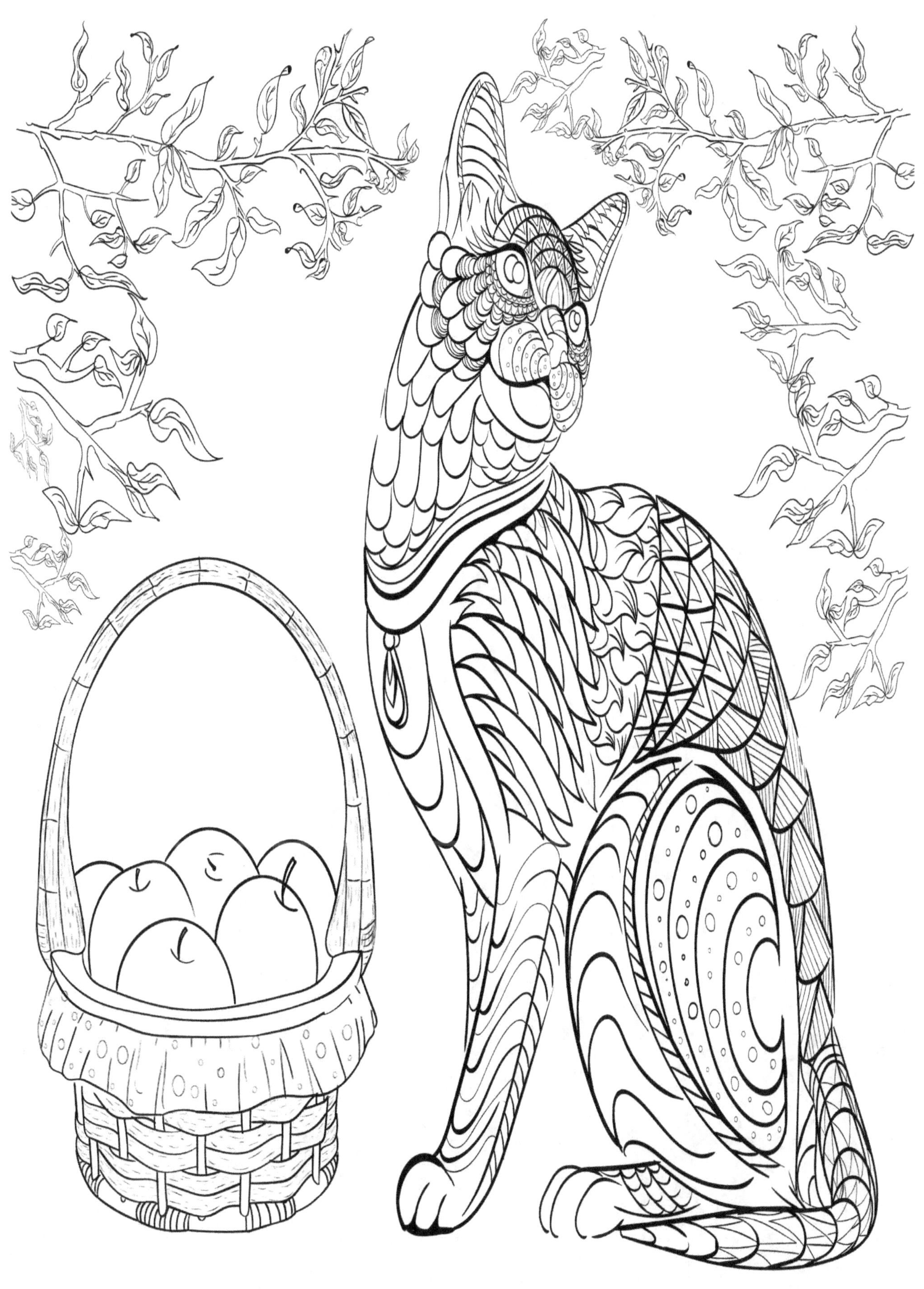

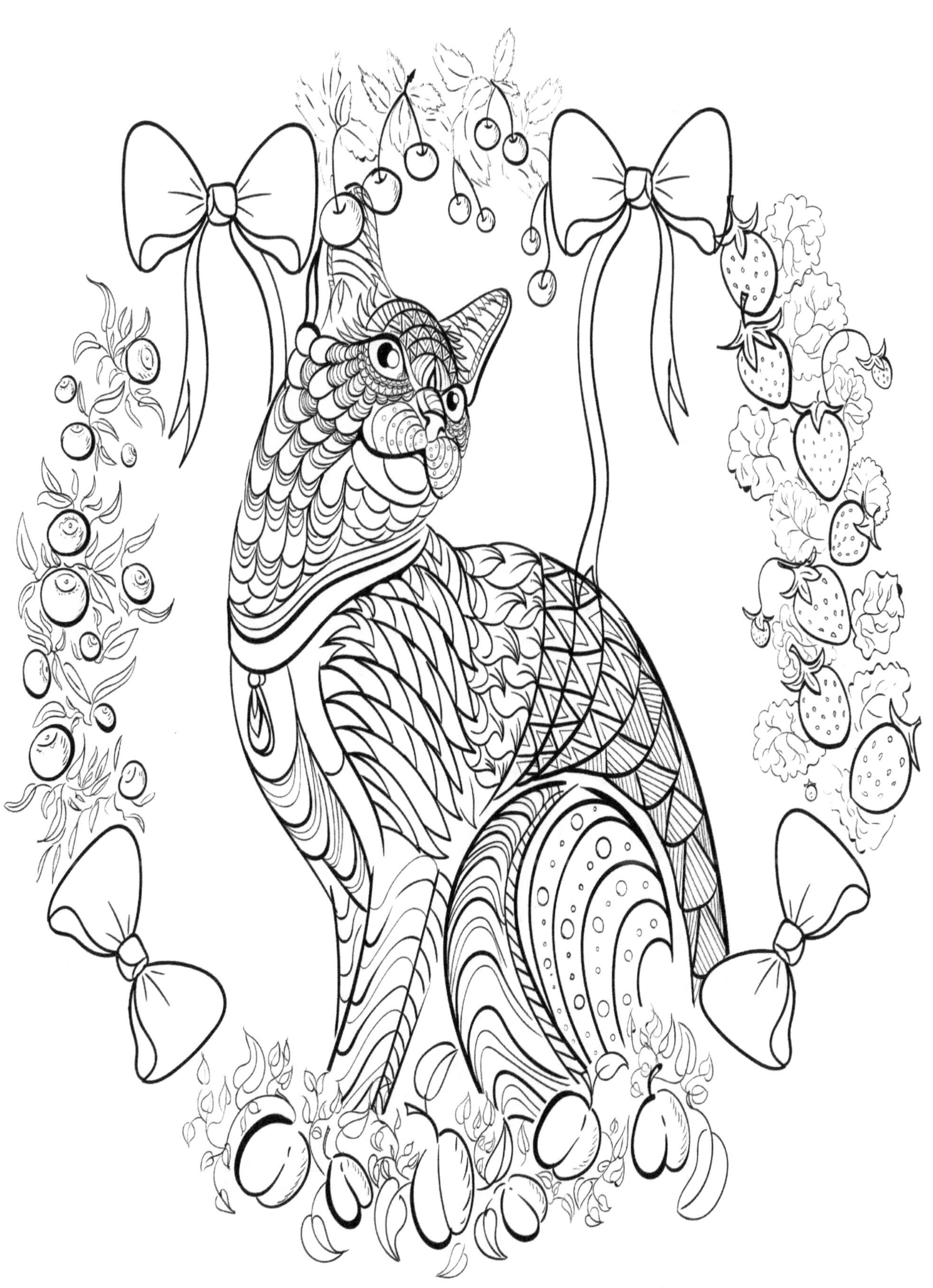

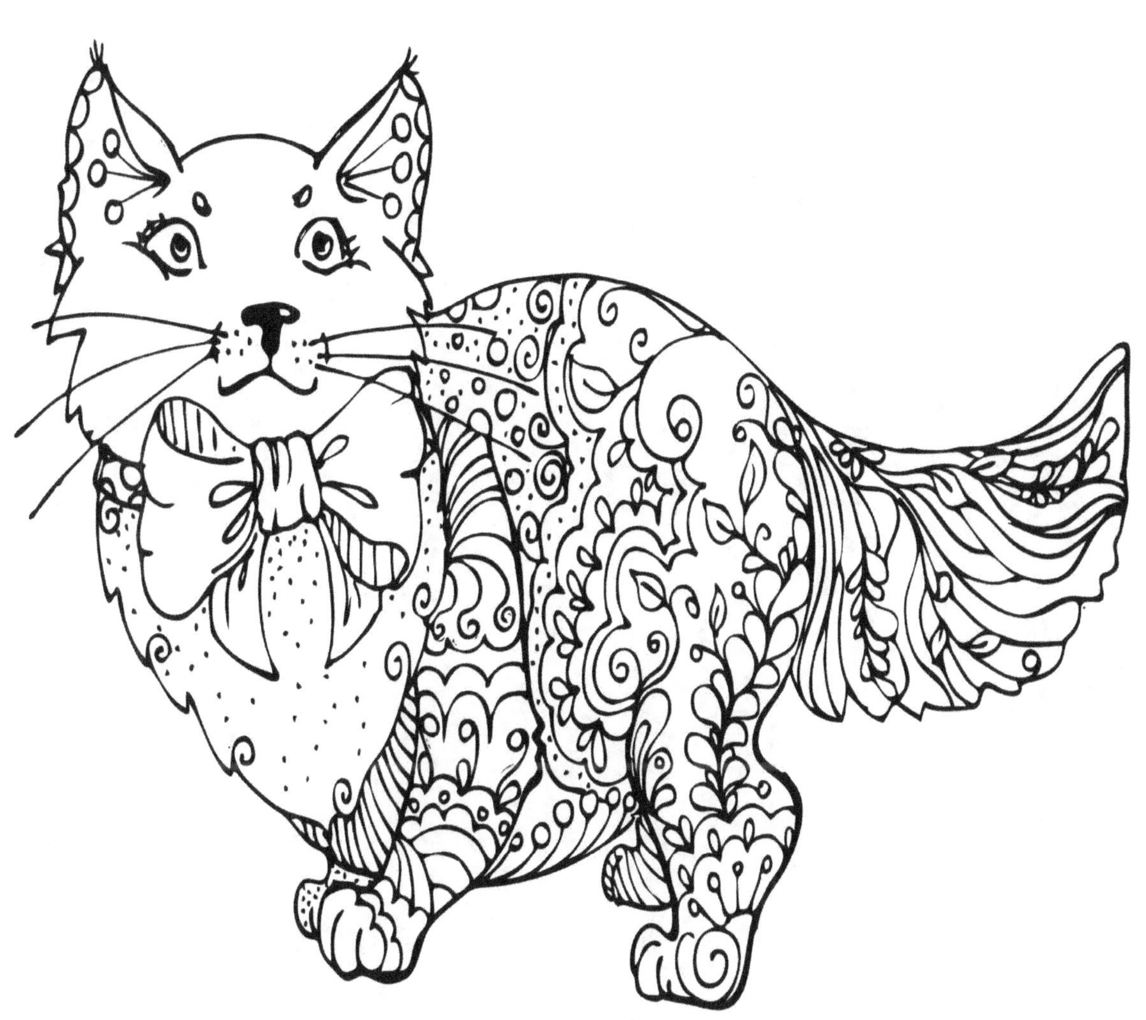

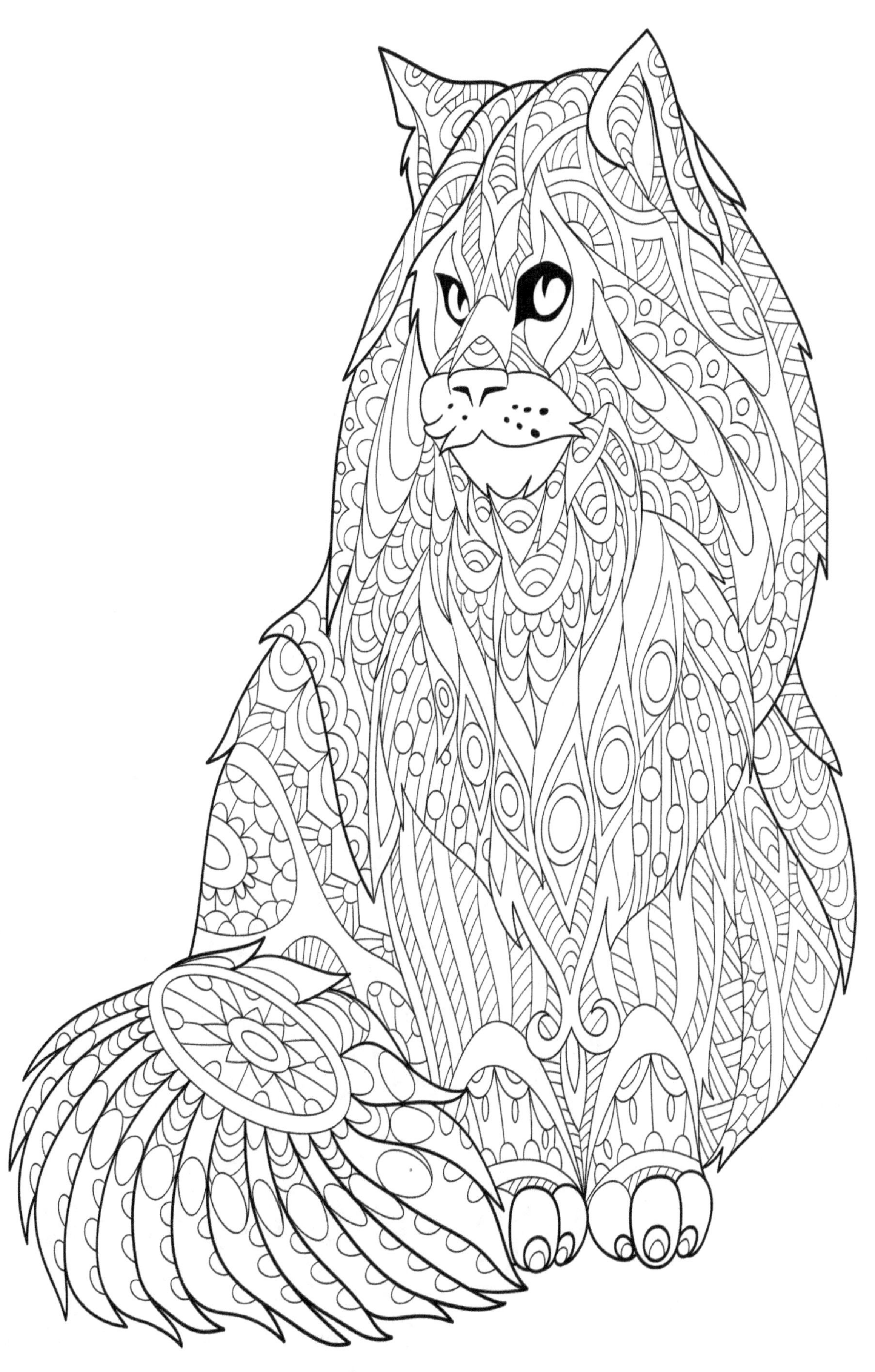

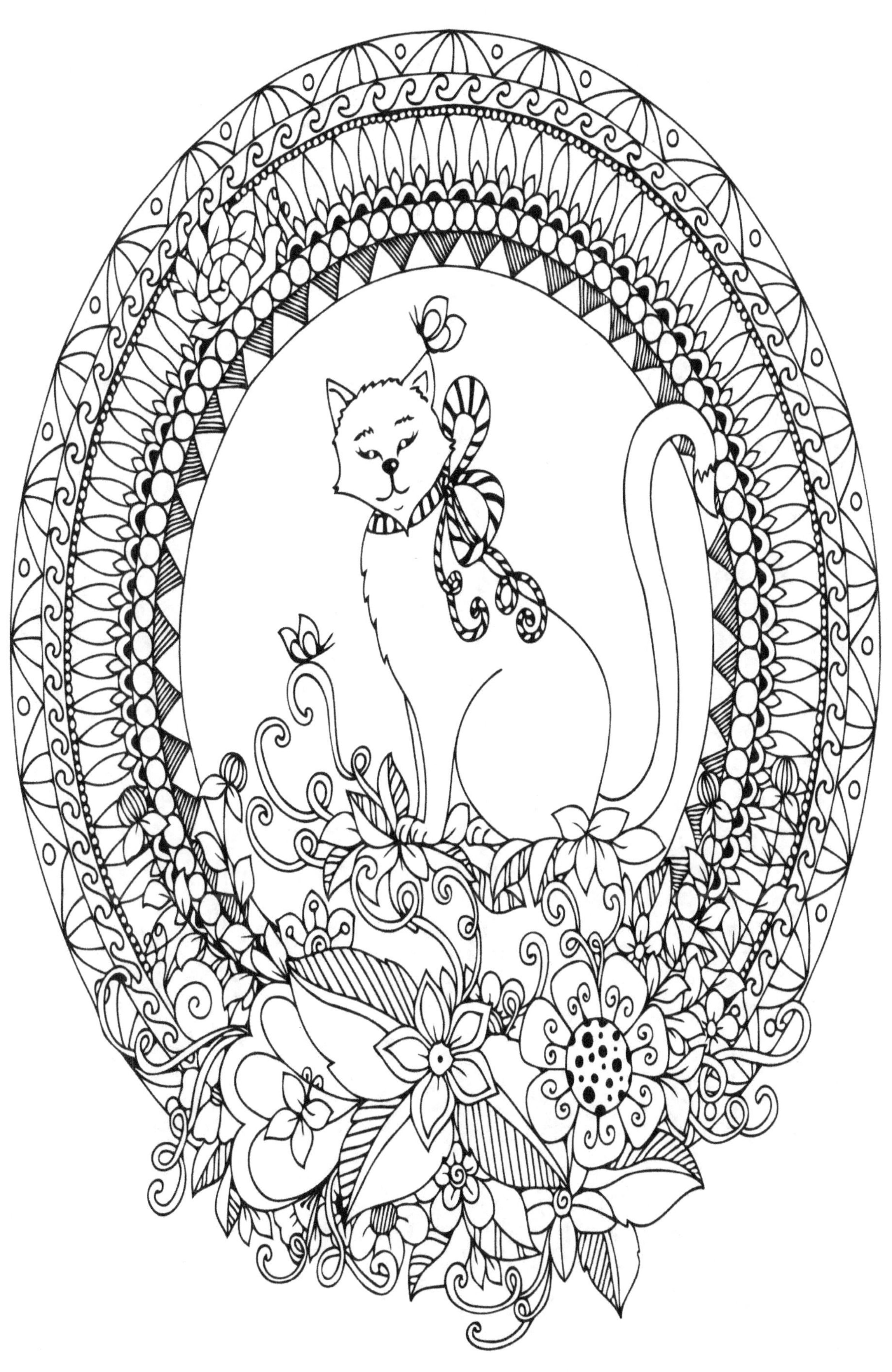

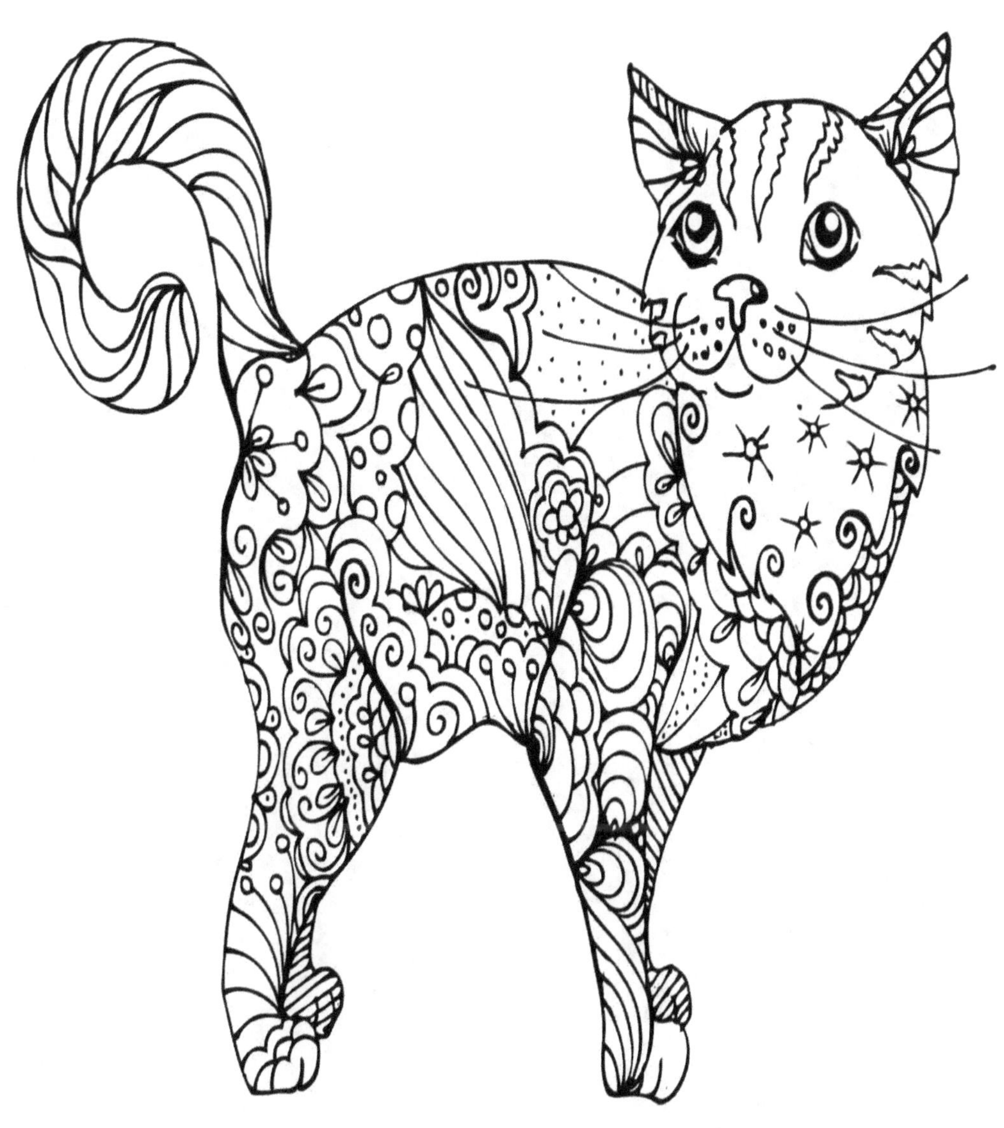

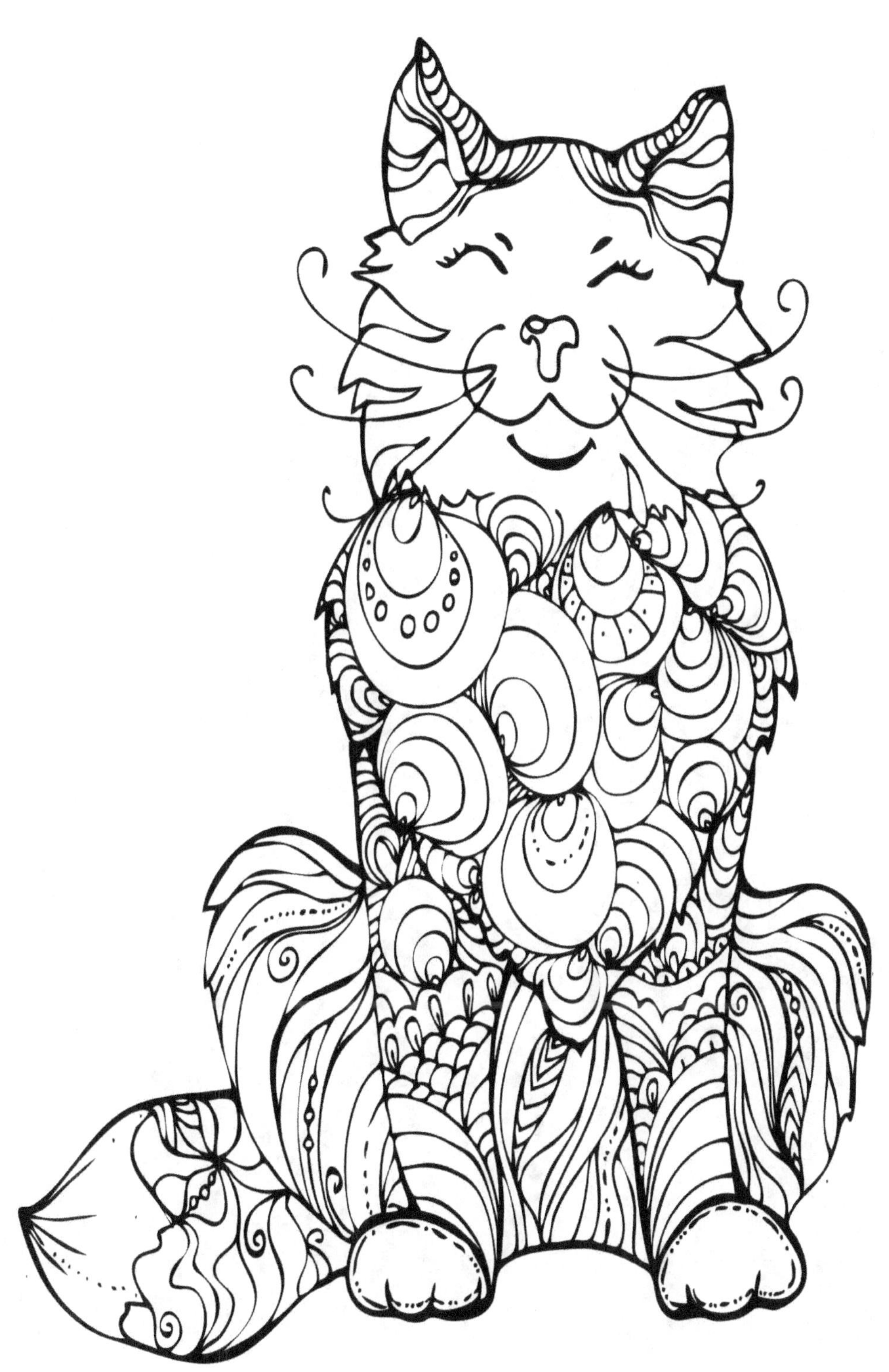

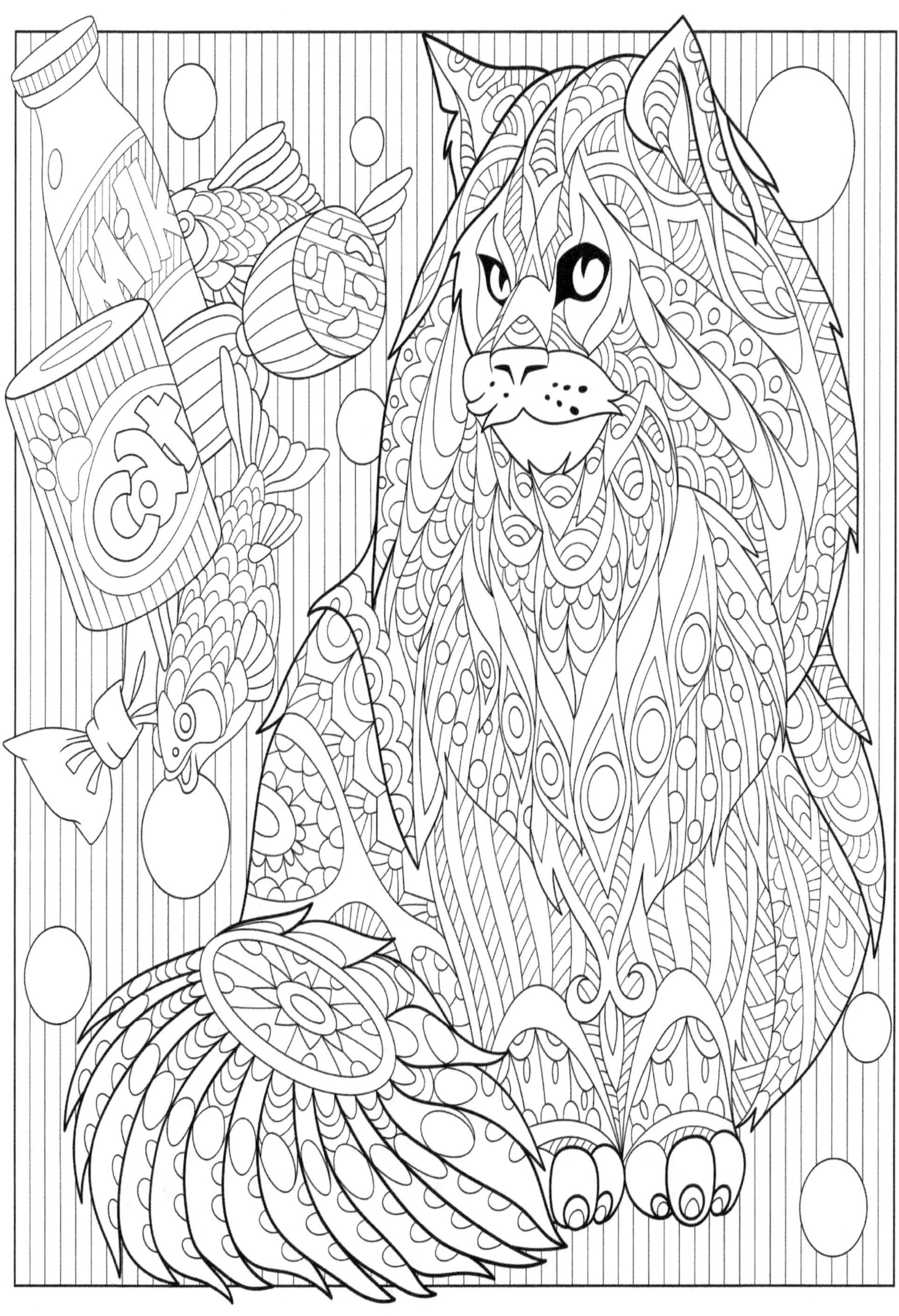
Milk
Cat

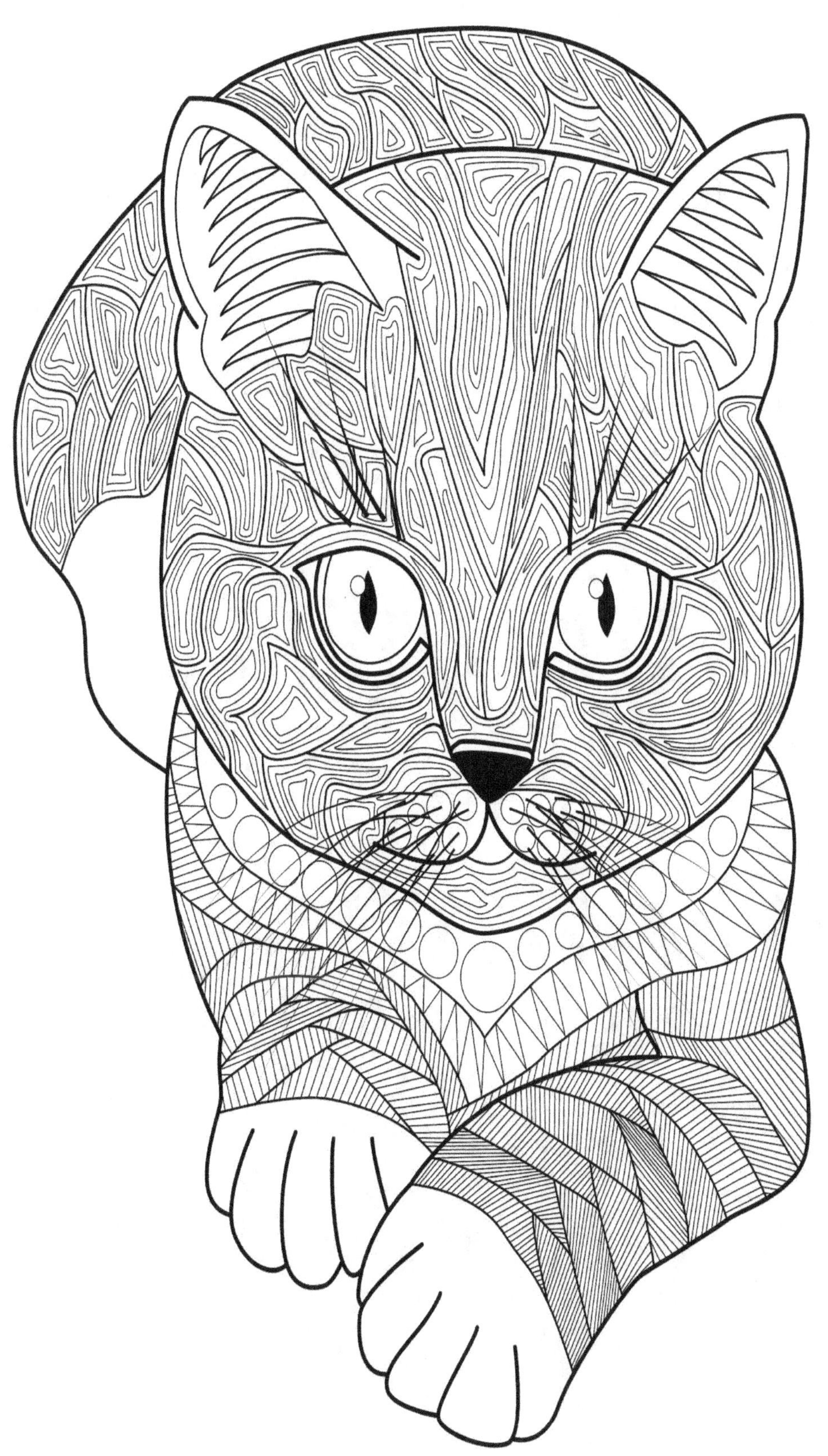

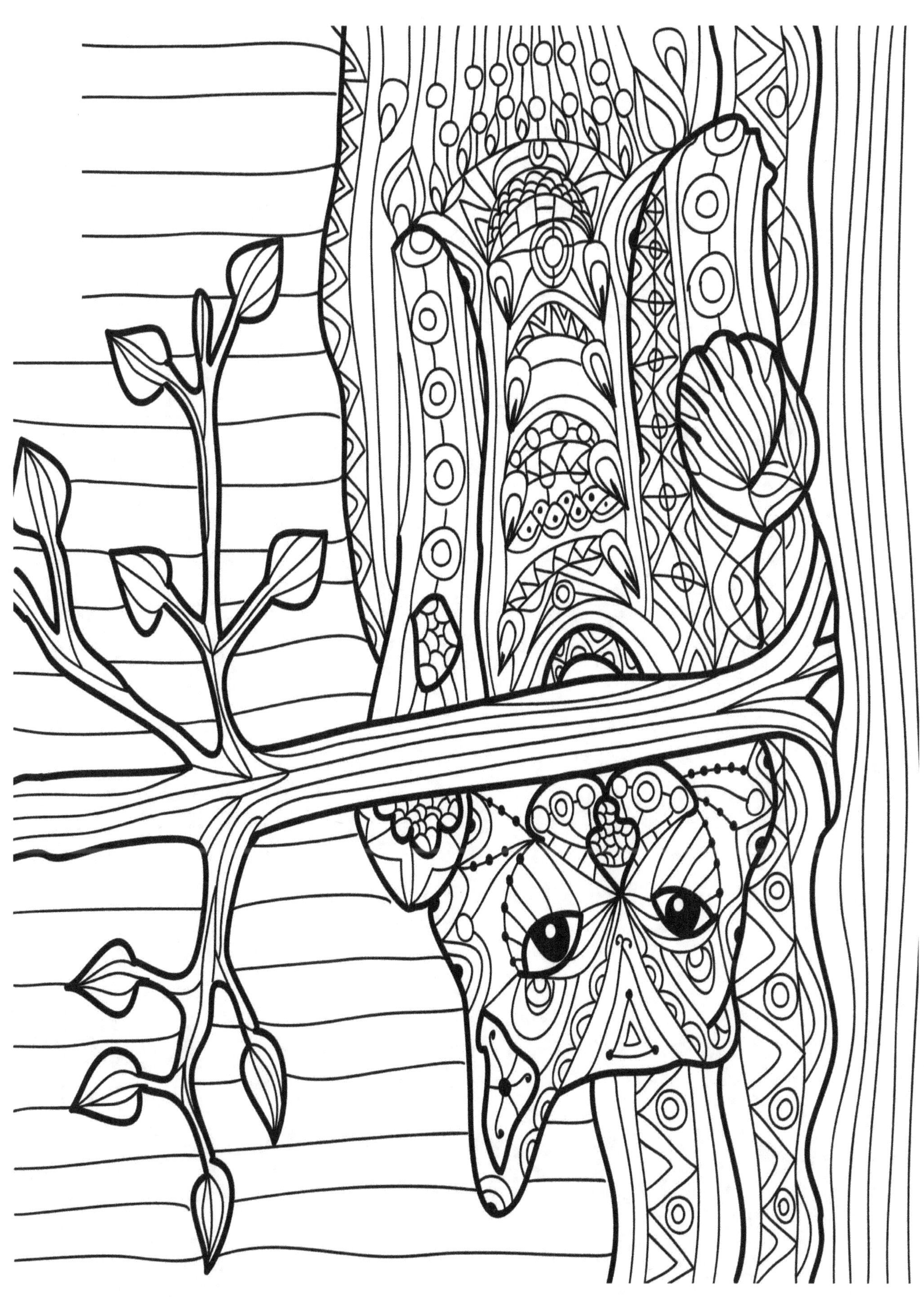

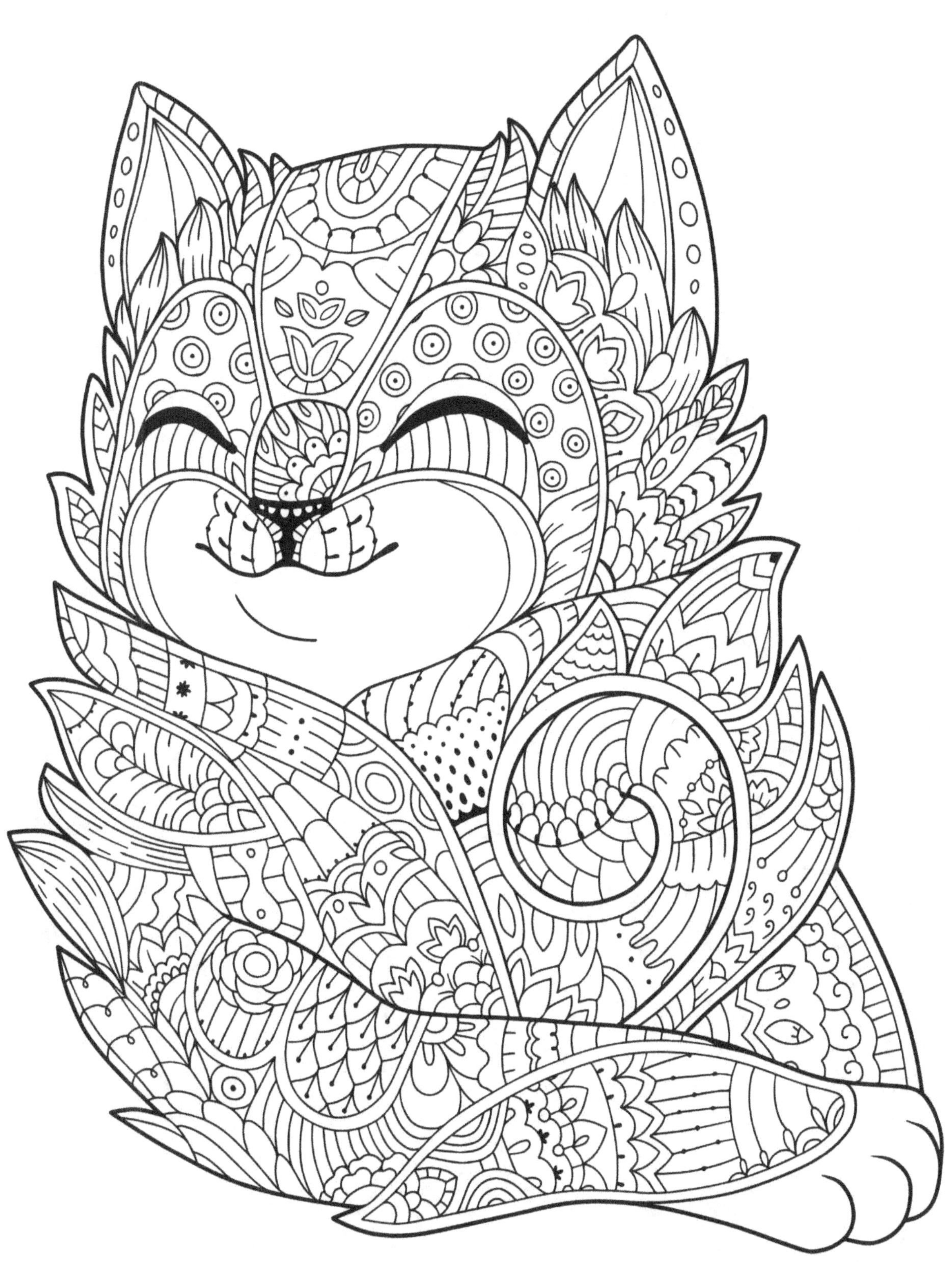

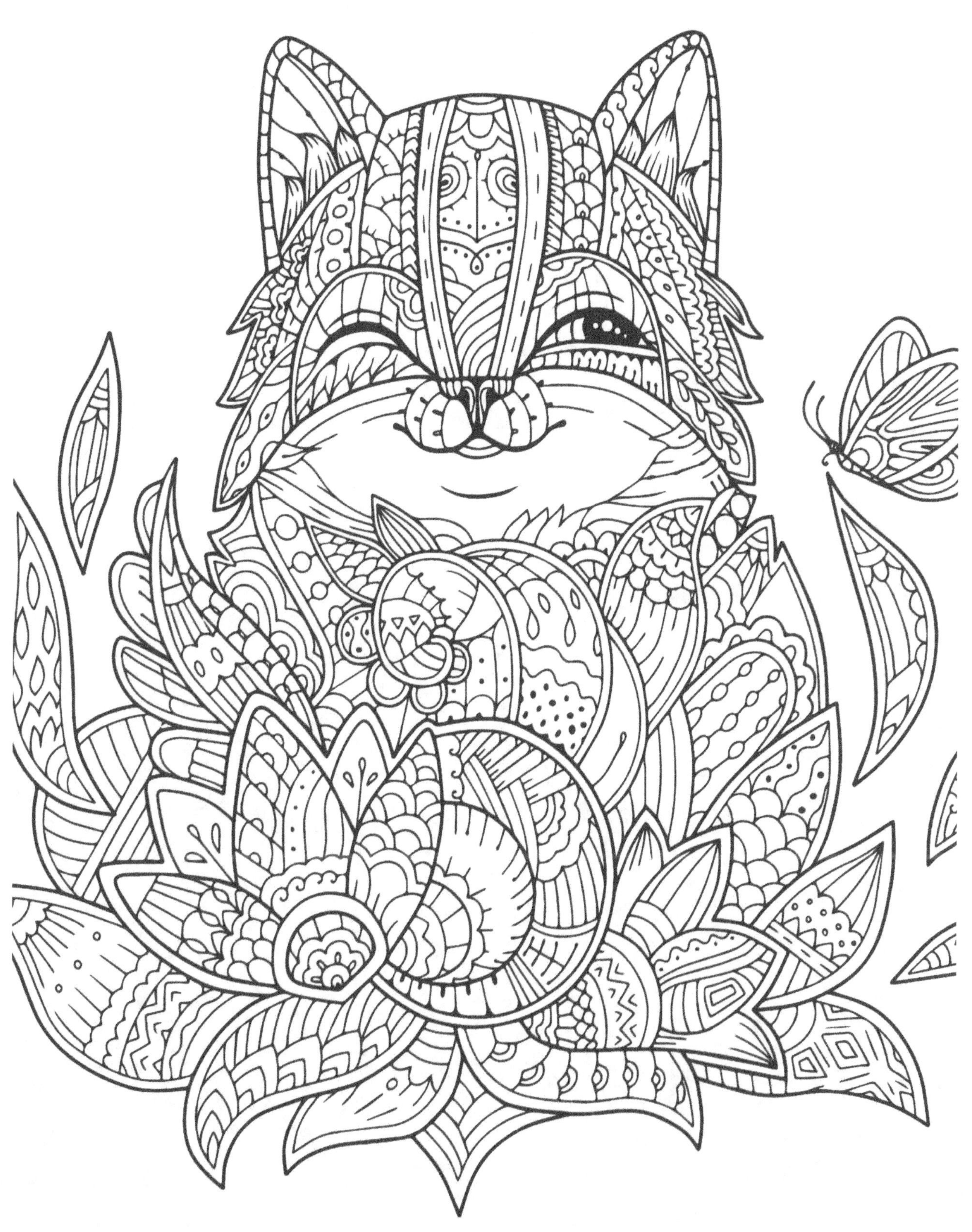

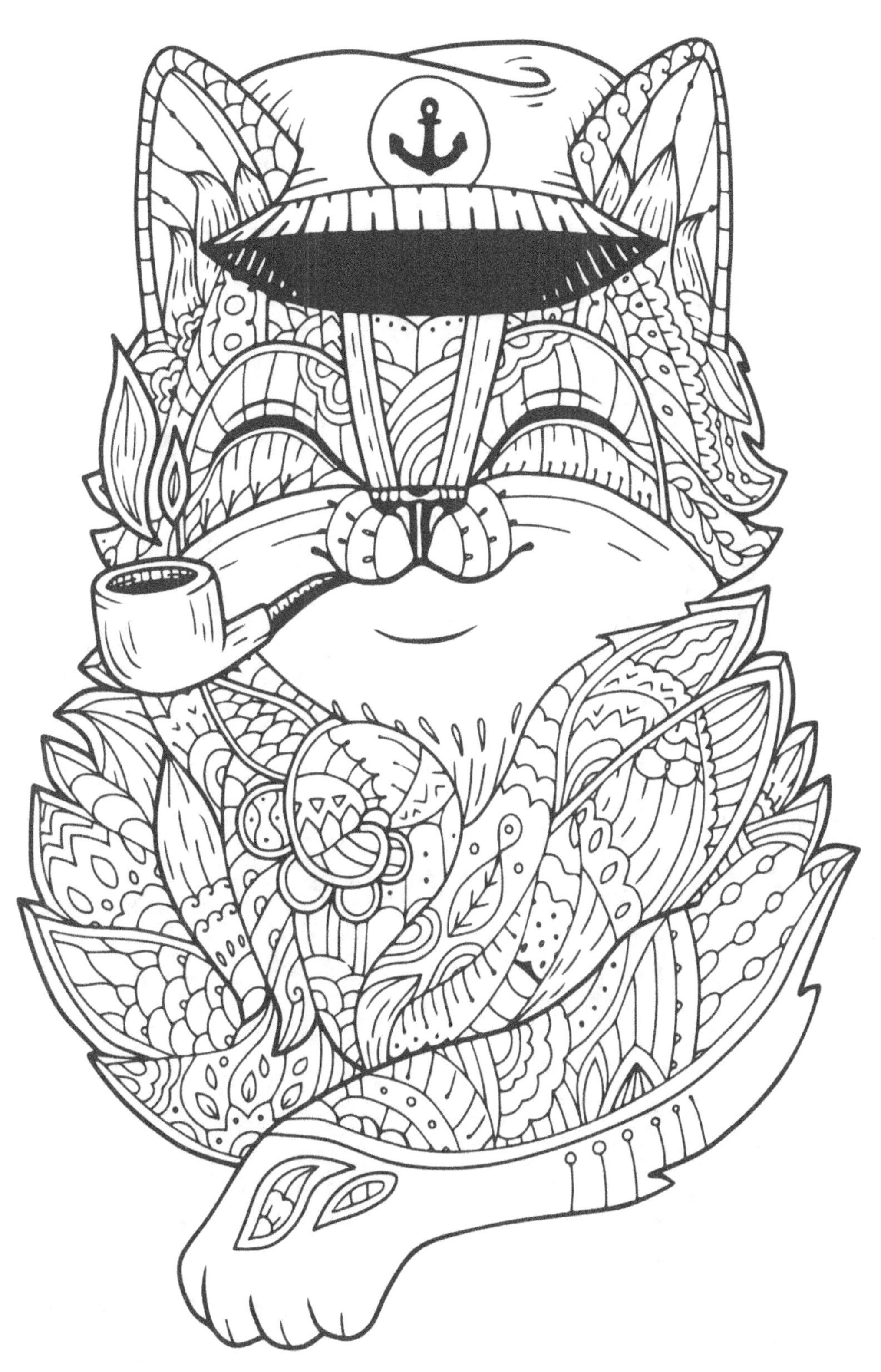

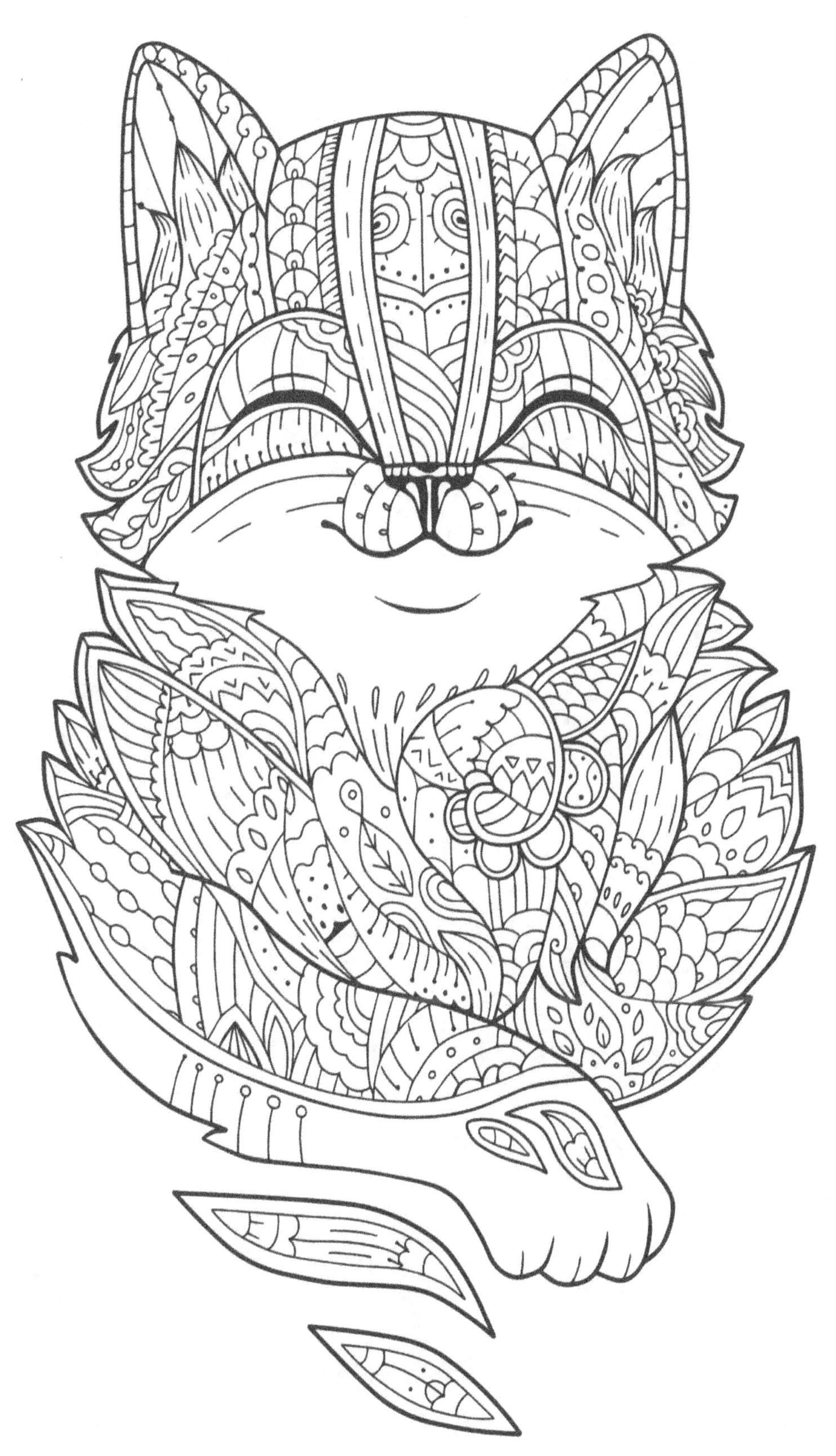

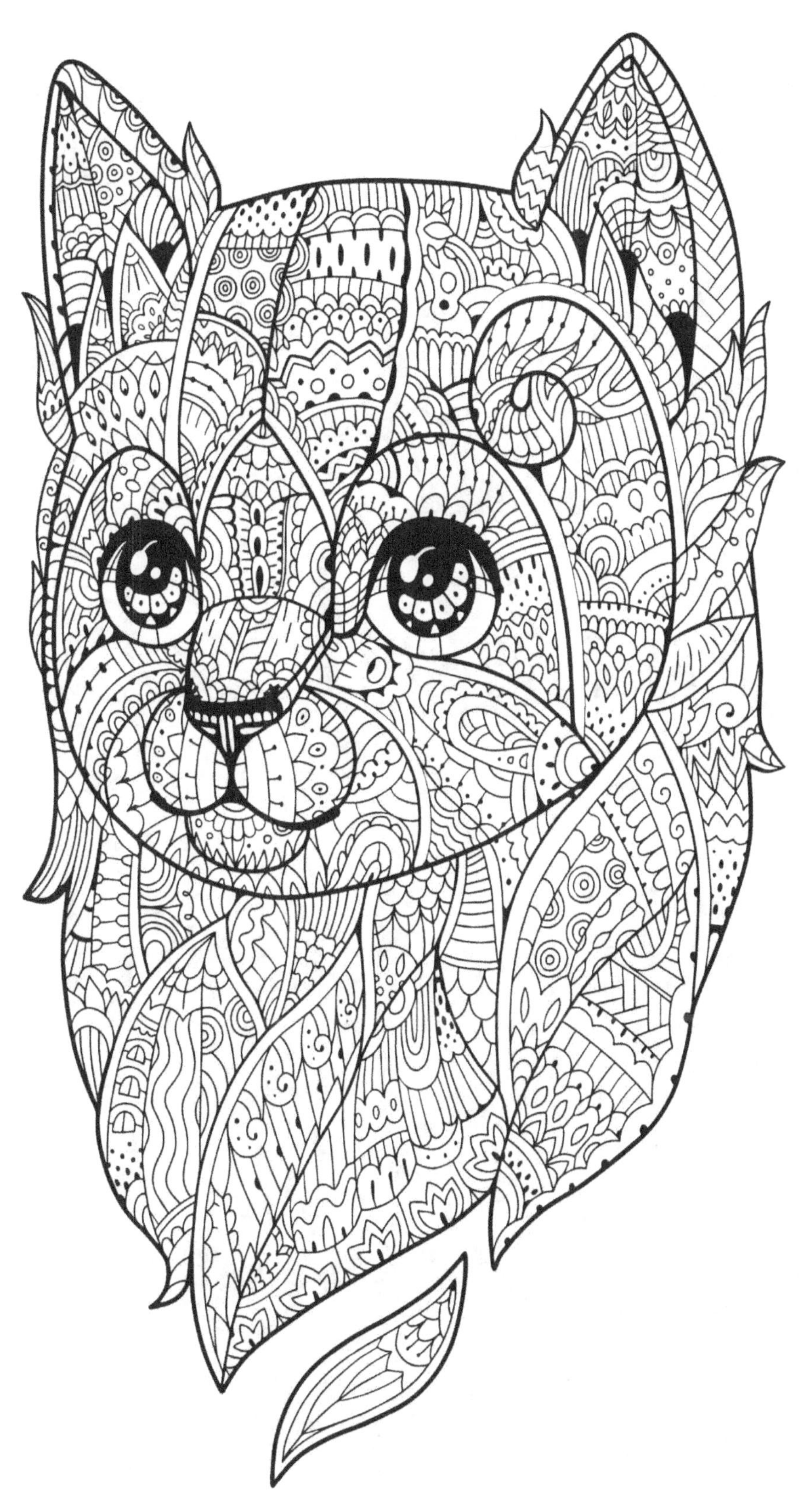

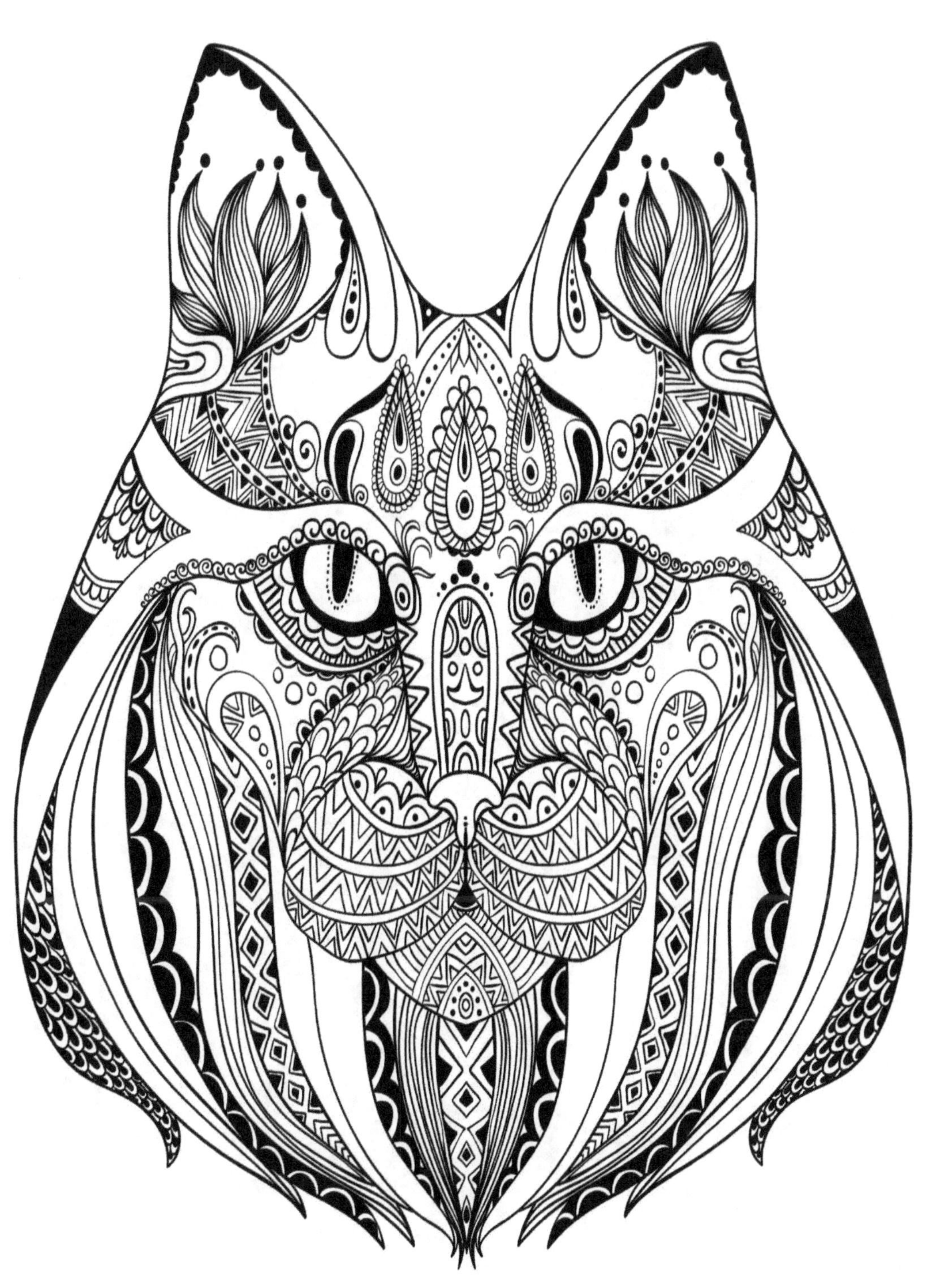

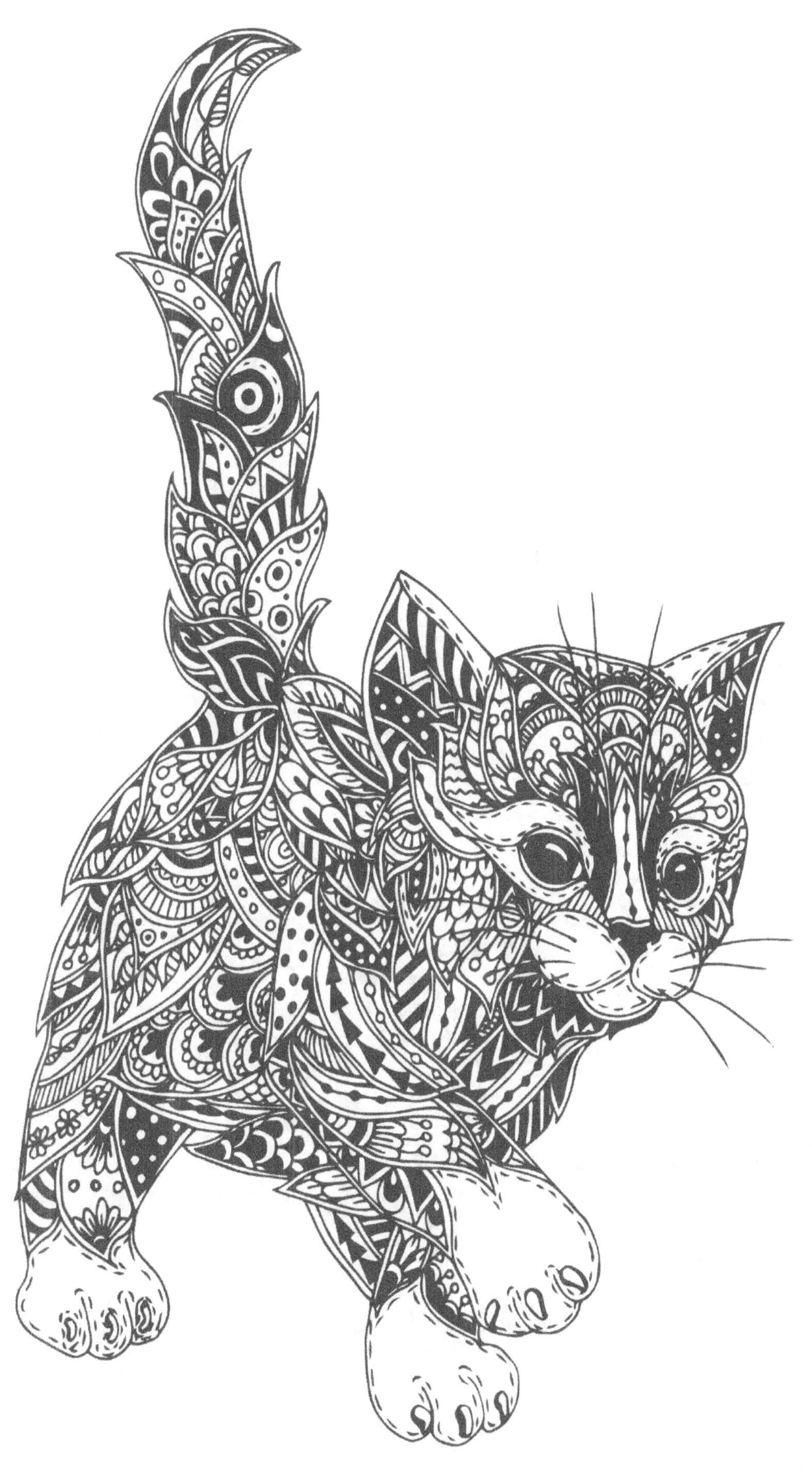

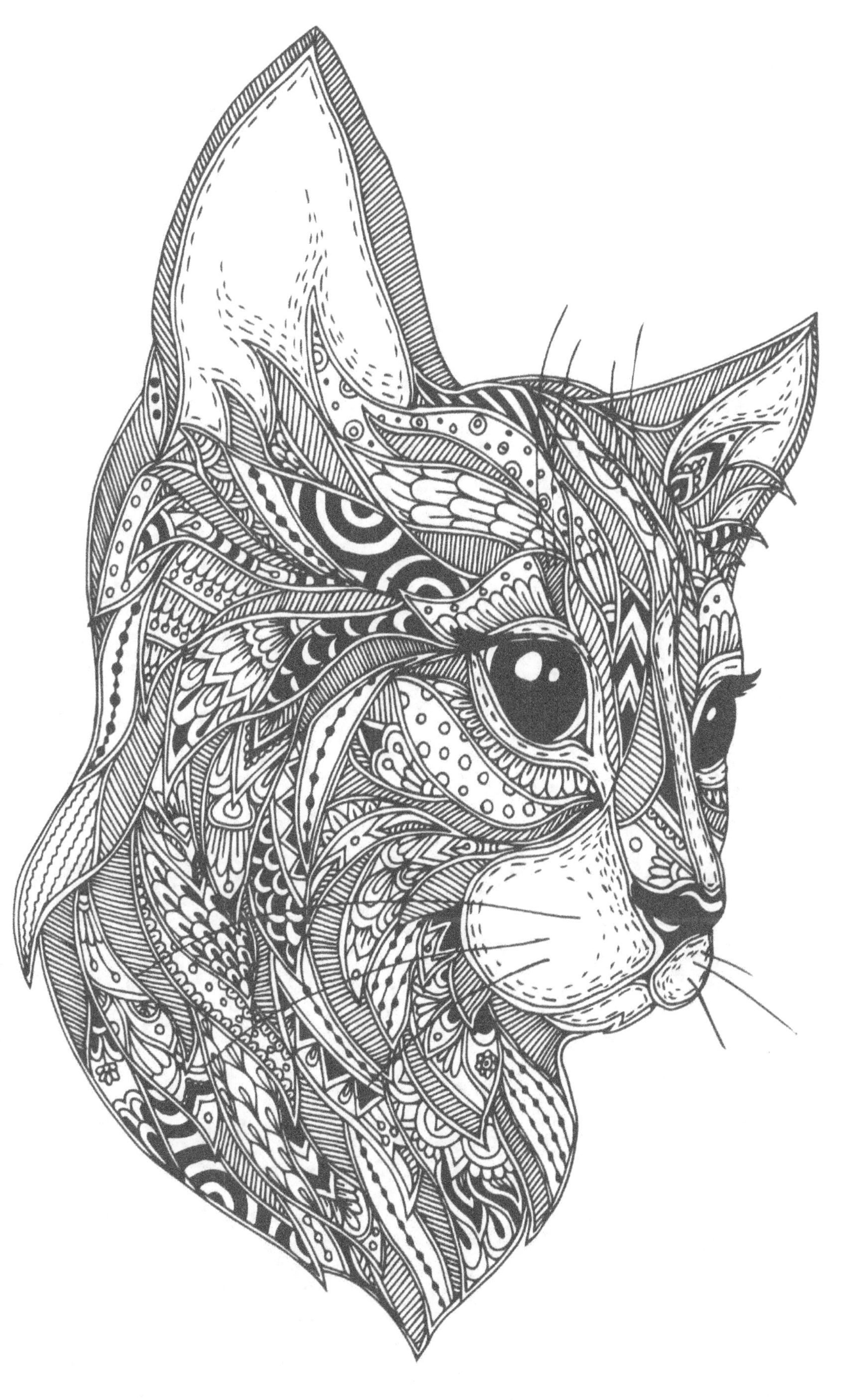

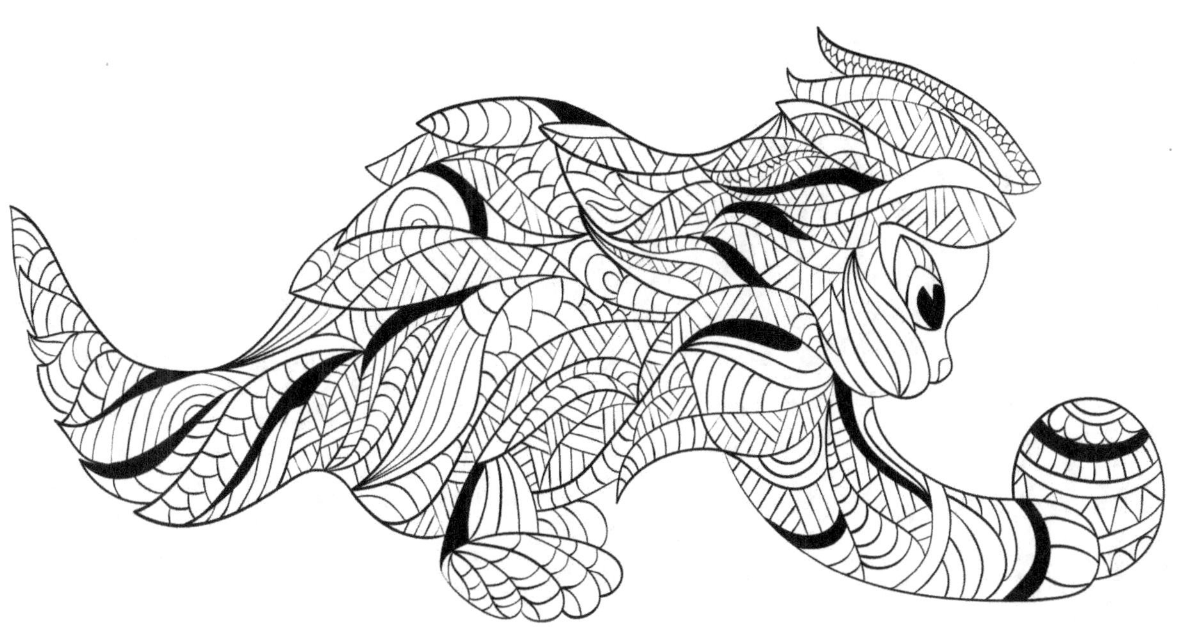

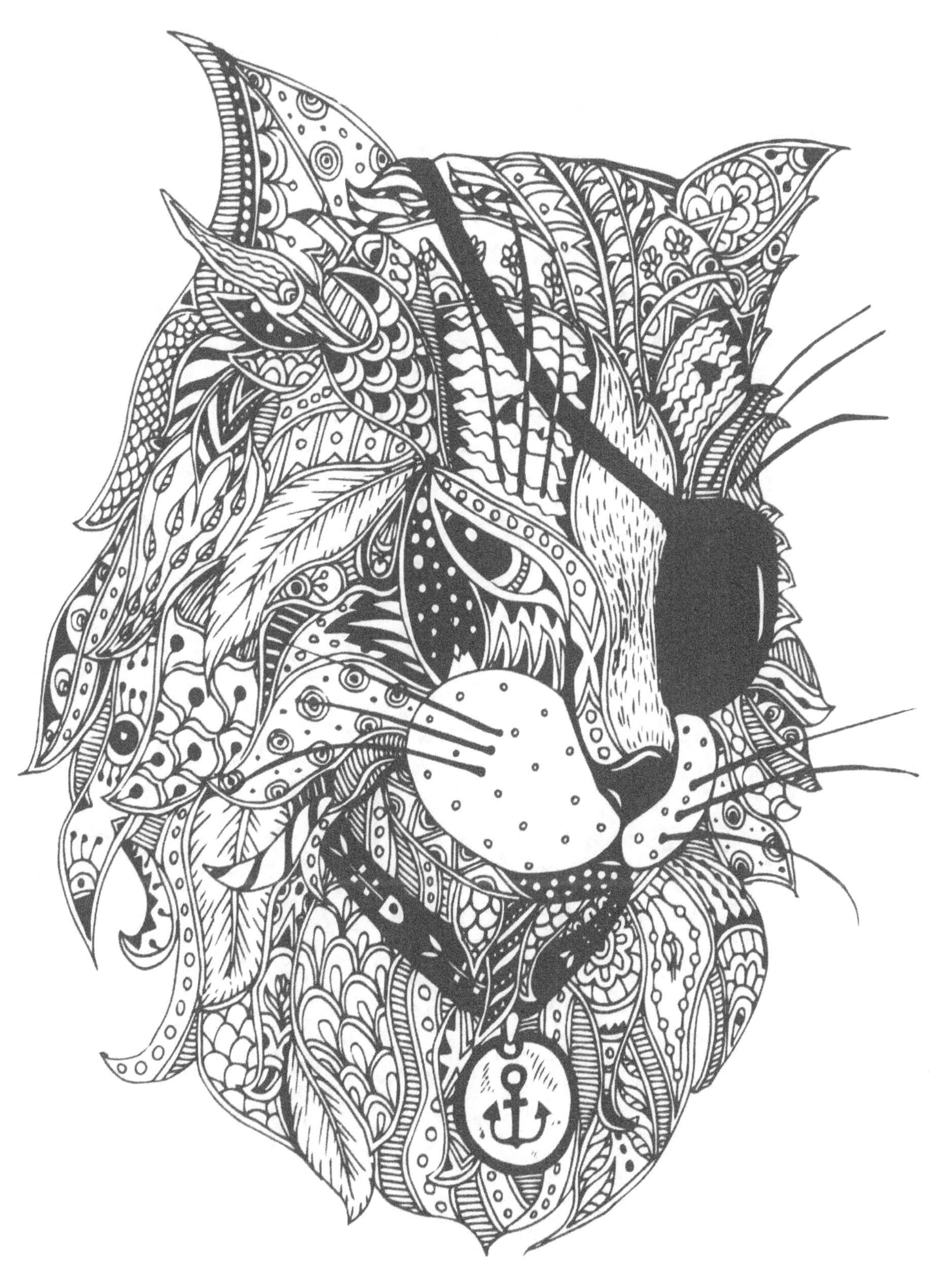